JENNIFER SERRAVALLO

New York Times best-selling author of *The Reading Strategies Book*

Teaching WRITING *in Small Groups*

HEINEMANN
Portsmouth, NH

Heinemann
361 Hanover Street
Portsmouth, NH 03801–3912
www.heinemann.com

Offices and agents throughout the world

The author and publisher wish to thank those who have generously given permission to reprint borrowed material:

Page 21: Excerpts from the Common Core State Standards. © Copyright 2010. National Governors Association Center for Best Practices and Council of Chief State School Officers. All rights reserved.

Library of Congress Control Number: 2020924811
ISBN: 978-0-325-13234-1

Editors: Katie Wood Ray and Zoë Ryder White
Production: Victoria Merecki
Cover and interior designs: Suzanne Heiser
Author photograph and interior photography: Nick Christoff and Michelle Baker
Interior art: © Deemak Daksina / Shutterstock (*bee icon*); © AVIcon / Shutterstock (*owl icon*)
Video editing: Michael Grover and Sherry Day
Typesetting: Gina Poirier Design
Manufacturing: Val Cooper

Printed in the United States of America on acid-free paper
1 2 3 4 5 6 7 8 9 10 BB 26 25 24 23 22 21
January 2021 Printing

This book is dedicated to
the teachers who showed up
physically, mentally, and
emotionally (whether through
a screen or in person) for
children and families every
day during the pandemic.
With unending gratitude
and awe, I see you.

Contents

PART I: Writing Small-Group Fundamentals

PART II: Types of Small Groups

Acknowledgments

Thanks first to my rock-solid editorial, design, production, and marketing teams at Heinemann. I do not ever take for granted how fortunate I am to collaborate with people who truly live up to the publisher's mission, and who are the perfect combination of exceedingly talented, always professional, and filled with heart. I couldn't have done this without you all:

- Katie Ray for your talent, steady guidance, and sharp eye

- Zoë Ryder White for pinch hitting with aplomb

- Suzanne Heiser for your flexibility, patience, and most of all incredible design

- Victoria Merecki for your consistent attention to every detail and keeping us all organized with such calm

- Sarah Fournier for lending your talents and fine-toothed comb

- Eric Chalek for your marketing prowess, loyalty, and dedication

- Heather Anderson for your work on the works cited

- Lauren Audet for spreading the word on social media

- and Stephanie George and Brett Whitmarsh for your incredible work on podcasts.

To Vicki Boyd and Roderick Spelman, thank you for making Heinemann such a fabulous home for my work and for your unwavering belief in me. I am endlessly grateful for your support.

Thank you to the students featured in the videos who were up for more Zoom school beyond their usual day, and their parents who said yes without hesitation when I asked if I could teach them some writing lessons online. Thanks also to Katie Thorn, Laurie Pandorf, and Toni Compel for resurrecting a year-plus-old video shot on a cell phone during a lab site and tracking down the families for permission. Michael Grover and Sherry Day and the rest of the video team—my thanks for making the videos so clear and accessible. Thanks also to the students who let me feature their work samples throughout this book, and Kristine Mraz for lending a few class-created samples.

Deep gratitude to my talented brother and sister-in-law—Nick Christoff and Michelle Baker—whose photography graces the pages of this book.

Thank you to my colleagues whom I lean on to be sounding boards, thought partners, and critical friends, especially: M. Colleen Cruz, Lainie Powell, Molly Wood, Lea Mercantini Liebowitz, Barbara Golub, Gina Dignon, and Rosie Maurantonio.

Thank you—above all and always—to my family.

About the Online Resources for This Book

In the online resources for this book you will find a variety of note-taking forms and videos that will help you get started with implementing—or refining—small-group writing instruction right away.

Skill-progression note-taking forms can help you identify goals for students, track progress, make in-the-moment decisions during small groups, and remind you of questions and prompts you can ask to learn more from your students. You can read more about how to use them in Chapter 2, and you'll see examples of them in use throughout the book.

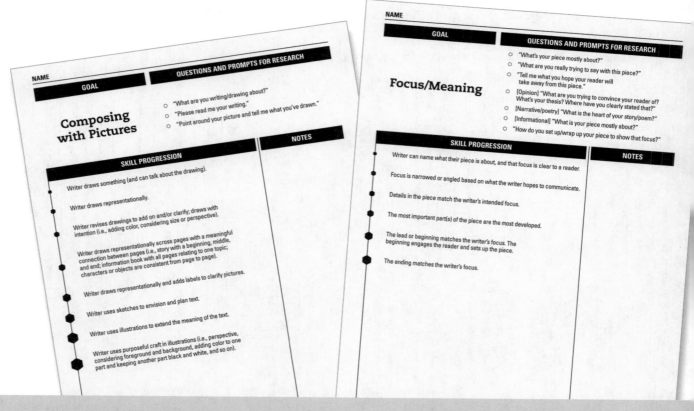

The videos I selected for this book were captured during a few different moments in time. Some of them were filmed before I had envisioned this book—they are examples of me teaching in first- and fourth-grade classrooms. I've used them in professional development with teachers over the past couple of years, and some of them appear in my Heinemann online course, Strategies in Action. About half of the videos were filmed during the COVID-19 pandemic using video-conferencing software. These were filmed with neighbors' children, friends of my daughters, and the children of friends across the country. I'm not their regular teacher, but they graciously agreed to be part of filming these examples.

An important note: *the teaching I describe in this book works whether you're in person in a physical classroom with children or you are working with them in an online "classroom."* Every video example you see that was filmed online could be conducted in person, and vice versa. As we get beyond this pandemic, I hope to get into a classroom or two with a video crew, film some additional examples, and upload the video to the online resources.

The one-on-one conferences and small groups feature students in grades K–8. I included individual conferences because they form a foundation for the types of small-group work described in the book. When you come upon a "Watch and Read" section (within Chapters 4–10) I encourage you to pause your reading and watch the video referenced, regardless of whether the age of students you teach matches the ages of the students in the video. The teaching moves you'll be invited to study are universal, and the video is meant to provide a key example of what's being described in the main text.

Below is a list of the conferences and small groups you'll be invited to view. In addition to these full-length lessons, there are also some short excerpts referenced in Chapter 3.

VIDEO CLIPS

CHAPTER	GRADE	LESSON TYPE	DESCRIPTION—GENRE AND GOAL(S)
4	1	Coaching conference	All-about books (informational), elaboration
4	4	Strategy lesson	Personal narrative, generating ideas
4	5	Student-led strategy lesson	Essay, elaboration
5	3	Guided writing	Persuasive letter, organization and structure
6	1	Shared writing	Poetry, elaboration
7	K	Interactive writing	Thank-you note, conventions
8	4	Inquiry conference	Narrative, conventions
8	7	Inquiry group	Narrative; elaboration, conventions, structure
9	4	Goal-setting conference	Narrative, elaboration
9	7	Reflection group	Poetry
10	1	Partnership conference	Narrative, giving feedback
10	4	Partnership conference	Narrative, oral storytelling/rehearsing

How to Access Online Resources

To access online resources for *Teaching Writing in Small Groups*:

1. Go to **http://hein.pub/WritingSmallGroups-login**.

2. Log in with your username and password. If you do not already have an account with Heinemann, you will need to create an account.

3. On the Welcome page, choose "Click here to register an Online Resource."

4. Register your product by entering the code: **TeachingWritingSG** (be sure to read and check the acknowledgment box under the keycode).

5. Once you have registered your product, it will appear alphabetically in your account list of My Online Resources.

Note: When returning to Heinemann.com to access your previously registered products, simply log into your Heinemann account and click on "View my registered Online Resources."

PART I

Writing Small-Group Fundamentals

THE CASE FOR
Small-Group Instruction in Writing

When and how do students write in school? What are the purposes for writing, and what procedures and processes do students follow when they write? Where does small-group instruction fit?

Consider Mr. Rivera's, Mr. De La Fuente's, and Ms. Walker's classrooms. As you read, notice how small-group instruction benefits students and teachers in every case, no matter the approach to writing instruction or grade level.

FROM CONFERRING TO SMALL GROUPS

Mr. Rivera describes himself as a "writing workshop teacher." He organizes his writing into monthlong units of study, each focused on a different genre. Every day, he teaches a very short whole-class lesson focused on one strategy, and then sends children off to write on topics they've self-selected. While children write, he makes his way around the classroom to confer with students one-on-one, something he's learned from studying Calkins, Graves, Murray, Atwell, and Anderson. He spends about five to seven minutes with each student checking to see

Continued on next page

FROM CONFERRING TO SMALL GROUPS
CONT.

Mr. Rivera *Continued from previous page*

how they are getting on with the class lessons and with strategies he's taught them in prior conferences, giving them targeted feedback on their writing, and offering them a strategy that will help them most today. He takes notes on each conference and follows up with students on past teaching. Some days children meet with writing partners, and most days the workshop ends with a gathering that he calls a "share" where students learn from each other.

Mr. Rivera loves the way he knows each of his writers. He feels confident that he's giving them support they need and he and his students enjoy the time they spend in conferences. What nags at him is how infrequently he's able to meet with students. In a class of twenty-eight fifth graders, with conferences averaging 5–7 minutes each plus a little time to travel from student to student and take some notes in between, it takes him seven class periods, or about a week and a half, to get back around to each student a second time. In that time, kids have often moved through multiple steps of the writing process, and many opportunities for individualized feedback have passed him by.

Incorporating small groups, and balancing small groups with individual conferring, will help him to maintain the valuable individualized instruction he's able to accomplish with conferring, but double the number of children he's able to see each week. He might start with one type of small group that feels like a conference—a strategy lesson—and pull a few children together at a time.

FROM THE WHOLE CLASS WITH THE SAME GOALS TO BALANCING INDIVIDUAL NEEDS

Mr. De La Fuente is trying to prepare his eighth graders for the sorts of academic writing they'll need to engage with next year in high school, specifically literary analysis and essay writing. He's painstakingly crafted a detailed rubric detailing what each student's piece needs to have, and he has offered a list of three thesis statements to choose from that align to the novel the students have just studied as a class. Each day, he gives a short lecture on one criteria from the rubric, and students work on a portion of their piece at their seats. While they work, he responds to raised hands, answering questions and giving help as students ask for it.

After a week, he asks all students to leave their drafts on his desk at the end of the class period. During lunch, as he looks through the drafts, he sees their needs run the gamut, although every student heard the same lecture each day. There seem to be a few that could use work on their introduction paragraphs. Several students still need to properly cite sources. Some are going on for way more sentences than necessary in each body paragraph, and it's cluttering the writing. Some seem to be including details from the text that aren't relevant, and it's muddying the focus of their piece.

He knows he's *taught* it all, but clearly they haven't all learned at the same pace. He offered to answer any questions that came up, but he realizes that it's likely that some didn't know enough about what issues they had in their writing to ask for help.

Incorporating small groups as students revise will allow him to target each area he's noticing students need support with, and go from having whole-class goals to finding individual goals for each student.

FROM WHOLE-CLASS SHARED PRACTICE TO SMALL-GROUP GUIDED PRACTICE

Ms. Walker believes in the power of writing instruction to help her first graders write better—and read better. She makes time every day for a whole-class lesson where her students help her compose a text. Some days they work on a new text; other days they return to previously written texts and make revisions and edits.

When teaching a writing lesson, she gathers her twenty-five first graders onto their classroom rug and directs their attention to the easel with chart paper. Sometimes she does all the writing, calling on children to give suggestions, or inviting them to turn and talk before sharing what a friend has said. Other times, she invites children up to write a letter or whole word on the chart. She feels that these shared and interactive writing lessons are very helpful in providing children with language models and examples of the genre they are practicing writing, and the students seem to enjoy them. But every day, she feels that although a portion of the children are completely with her, there are some who are bored (they know all the things she's pointing out and could just write it on their own) and others are confused (the lesson is moving too fast, or the sorts of strategies they are practicing aren't within their current grasp). When she sends children off to do some of their own writing, she sees her lessons stick for a portion of the class, but she knows many children need something else.

Incorporating small groups during the time when children are doing their own writing, and balancing these small groups with some of the whole-class lessons she has children engage in, will allow her to more carefully fine-tune and target what students need. They will get more support and specialized feedback on their specific pieces of writing and their strategies and processes. She can even use some of the same methods—shared writing and interactive writing—in small groups, and also try out some new methods for different purposes.

Small-Group Writing Instruction Allows Teachers and Students To . . .

Value Each Child's Language and Literacy Practices

Most classrooms today are filled with children who have a rich diversity of language and literacy practices. When instruction is always whole class, it's easy for that richness to become less visible as all children try to conform to a single standard. Working with children in small groups gives you the opportunity to tailor instruction to each child as a unique and competent learner, valuing and affirming the language and literacy practices of each (España and Herrera 2020; Ladson-Billings 2009; Souto-Manning and Martell 2016).

Develop Relationships

Positive relationships between teacher and students are a precursor for learning to happen (Howard, Milner-McCall, and Howard 2020; Hammond 2015; Minor 2018). When you work to build relationships, your small groups will be more beneficial for you and your students. Also, working with children in small groups (and one-on-one) can *help to strengthen* relationships.

Simply putting children into small groups does not automatically mean that a positive relationship will result, but working with children in groups in ways described in this book—ways that allow for two-way feedback with lots of listening on the part of the teacher, that offer support for strategies that are meaningful and appropriate, that invite true collaboration, and that show true caring from the teacher who communicates with body language and words "You've got this!"—can help move toward the goal.

Teach and Learn with Efficiency

There are only so many minutes in a day, and only so many minutes each week you can devote to writing instruction and writing practice for your students. Ideally, you're able to find four or five class periods of forty-five to sixty minutes each week where children participate in some whole-class instruction followed by independent writing time with conferring and small-group instruction. Let's say we have thirty minutes five times a week, or 150 minutes weekly, for conferring and small-group time. If you were to do only one-to-one conferring, assuming an average of five minutes per conference, that means you could do *thirty* conferences. (My class sizes in New York City when I was an elementary teacher were a little over thirty students, so I wouldn't get to every student even once a week with only individual conferences.)

If instead you shifted to small-group instruction only, and you are able to see three children in a seven- to ten-minute small group (for the purposes of estimating, let's just say ten minutes per group), then you'd be able to do fifteen small groups times three children in a group—that's forty-five children a week (or twenty-two children twice a week) who receive targeted instruction and feedback.

In all likelihood, you'll use a *balance* of methods—sometimes groups, sometimes conferences. Sometimes your groups will be two children, sometimes four. But the point is this: using small-group instruction alongside conferring makes it possible for you to meet with *every student once or twice a week* to give individualized support about their writing during writing time.

Increase Engagement

When moving from mostly whole-class instruction to more small-group instruction, you'll notice an uptick in engagement and attentional focus on the part of the learners. Their physical proximity to you, and the amount of one-to-one interactions that are possible as you ask them questions, nudge their thinking, or prompt them as they try, increases dramatically. You'll read more about feedback in Chapter 3, but for now consider this tidbit from neuroscientist James Zull as cited in Hammond (2015): receiving feedback triggers the brain to release *dopamine*, which motivates a student to work harder and persevere. When students apply feedback, it stimulates the growth of neurons and dendrites and grows more gray matter. Moving from all whole-class to small-group instruction increases the number of times you are able to offer children specific, helpful, actionable feedback and will literally grow and change their brain and help them to be more engaged in their own learning (Hammond 2015). For those of you reading who already have lots of individualized instruction in the form of conferences, doing more small groups will help you see more children in a class period, increasing the number of moments across a week when children are engaged in the feedback cycle with you.

Improve Independence

It can be easy for children to get lost if lessons are only whole class—with a wide range of learners, the teaching in a whole-class setting can only be "just right" for a portion at any given time. This is true in any subject area! When you incorporate small-group instruction as a regular part of your schedule, you're able to offer strategies in the context of student goals—what they *want* to and *need* to be working on. That alone makes the instruction meaningful and engaging. But in small groups you also can provide feedback in the moment, support students with practice, and make sure they "get it" (or at least get *closer* to "it") before they continue independently with their work. They will take on new learning more quickly and better be able to continue independently.

Develop Social Support Among Students

Both within and during the small groups you lead, and then during classroom time as children continue to write independently, students can look to peers as other learners who are working on the same goals, skills, and strategies. Within groups, they might overhear you giving feedback to a friend, which they can then apply to their work. They might hear a child share an example of a place in their writing where they successfully applied a strategy, which becomes another model for them as they work on their own writing. This is built-in support for learners. In addition, as children begin to get the hang of strategies and accomplish goals, they can be class experts on topics and can be leaders of their own small groups (see more about student-led small groups in Chapters 4 and 8).

Give and Receive Feedback

Grouping children allows us to *give* more feedback, but just as importantly it allows us to *get* feedback. The feedback we receive from students about our teaching is crucial to be able to revise, adapt, pivot, and change to positively impact learning outcomes (Hattie 2008). When we group kids, it can blur the line between teacher and student in the best of ways—you become a researcher as you learn about your students and they learn from you, and you cocreate knowledge alongside your students (Morrell 2012; Freire 1998). You can read more about what to watch for, and how to ask for feedback from your students, in Chapter 3.

So What Is the Rest of the Class Doing?

By now I hope you're convinced that small-group work can enhance any classroom, whether the intention is to move from strictly whole-class instruction to groups or to balance groups with one-to-one conferring, whether you teach kindergarten or seventh grade. When looking at your packed schedule, you might wonder "How do I fit this in?" and "What is the rest of the class doing?"

The short answer is: the rest of the class is writing, and you fit your groups in during a time when they write. As Stephen King writes, "You cannot succeed unless you read a lot and write a lot. It's not just a question of how-to, you see; it's a question of how much to. Reading will help you answer how much, and only reams of writing will help you with the how. You can learn only by doing" (2000, 173).

This writing time might be its own class period or a portion of an English language arts block or could even happen during content areas (science, social studies) when children are independently writing about a topic under study. Children need to be engaged independently in their work or working with a partner or small group in collaboration without the need for teacher involvement for you to be freed up to work with them in groups; importantly, they also need independent work time when you're not meeting with them to have plenty of time to practice and apply what you've taught during the group and other lessons.

How much time? It depends on your schedule, but remember that for you to meet with children regularly, they need regular blocks of time to write. In my elementary classroom, I taught writing four days a week and usually blocked out about an hour: forty-five minutes of which was used for conferring and small-group instruction with some time spent in whole-class instruction (minilessons or studying a mentor text). As a consultant, I work with middle school teachers who have under an hour for English language arts, which must include both reading *and* writing, so they either choose to split their class time each day, teach reading or writing every other day, or focus on each for a mini-unit: reading for a week (or longer), then switching to writing for a week (or longer).

When you look at your overall schedule, my advice is to go for balance. Balance of reading and writing. Balance of a (small amount) of whole-class instruction followed by a large chunk of time when kids can write and you can confer and work with small groups.

TAKE IT TO YOUR
CLASSROOM

✓ Reflect on how you currently balance whole-class lessons with small-group or one-on-one instruction.

✓ Consider your students' level of engagement and the amount of and frequency of individual feedback. How might your students and you benefit from small-group instruction?

✓ To make time and space for small-group instruction in your classroom, reflect on what you might need to adjust or change in your daily or weekly schedule.

"Working with children in small groups gives you the opportunity to tailor instruction to each child as a unique and competent learner, valuing and affirming the language and literacy practices of each."

Forming Groups

For small-group instruction to be successful students first need to belong together in the same group, and second, they need a type of group and method of instruction that will set them up to practice what they need. Therefore, you'll need to be comfortable with assessing and evaluating student work to identify what each student should focus on (a goal), and then monitor progress as they learn (using skill progressions). By regarding every small-group lesson as not only a chance to teach and guide students, but also as a chance to check in and assess, you'll be ready to move children flexibly from group to group, or from groups to individual conferences and back again, always responding to their needs.

Your teaching will be most effective when it focuses on what each individual student needs, holds everyone to high but realistic expectations, and communicates your belief in their ability to succeed. To grow, they will need opportunities for productive struggle—the work should be not so challenging that it's frustrating or goes over their heads and not so easy that they aren't learning from it (Howard, Milner-McCall, and Howard 2020; Milner 2010; Hammond 2015; Ritchart 2002; Means and Knapp 1991).

In this chapter, you'll read about these four steps to make assessment—both initial and ongoing—second nature and to help you choose the right type of small group with confidence:

✅ **Step 1:** Identify a goal.

✅ **Step 2:** Use skill progressions to see growth opportunities within goals.

✅ **Step 3:** Monitor progress with skill progressions and adjust as needed.

✅ **Step 4:** Choose a group type.

Step 1: Identify a Goal

Small-group instruction is manageable, and progress is faster, when your teaching and each student's practice is centered around a predictable goal (Hattie 2008). Having a clear list of goals—and an order in which to tackle them—can help aid in decision making for you and your students.

Below is my hierarchy of goals for writing, first published in *The Writing Strategies Book* (Serravallo 2017). This list of goals can help you categorize and organize your thinking about writing habits and qualities of good writing. Although all the goals in the hierarchy are equally important, and you'll want to develop all areas for every writer, they are arranged in an intentional order: goals to address first are at the top and goals to address later are at the bottom, so that it is easier to focus on one thing at a time.

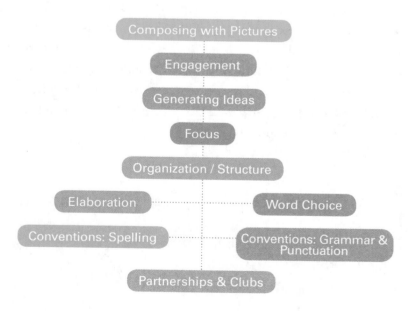

When you assess student writing and habits, look at the student's work and consider the goals on the hierarchy from top to bottom. The first place you see an opportunity to support the student is the goal you can choose to focus on for some time, until they've learned a few strategies toward that goal and have become independent using them.

In the following chart is a list of the goals, a brief description of each, and some general advice for what to look for when observing as students write, listen for as they talk about their writing, or notice when reading or looking at their written work (both words and drawings).

Download the goals chart. See page xiii for instructions.

GOAL	DESCRIPTION
Composing with pictures	**What is this goal?** Using pictures on their own or in conjunction with print to communicate meaning. Using pictures to plan before writing or to illustrate after writing. **Look for:** • How pictures are used (to plan, to add more after writing, as stand-alone text without words) • Evidence of revision of pictures • Ability to connect pages • Amount of detail used in pictures • Whether pictures are readable to others
Engagement	**What is this goal?** Enjoying writing, having attentional focus required to write for a sustained period of time. **Look for:** • The quantity of writing produced in a sitting • Outward signs of attention and focus during writing time • How a writer describes their attitude toward writing • Whether a writer chooses to write, or only does it when assigned
Generating ideas	**What is this goal?** Coming up with and/or collecting ideas for what to write about. Finding a unique angle if a topic is assigned. Having a passion or an interest in topic(s) they choose. **Look for:** • A writer's ability to come up with a topic and start writing • A writer's enthusiasm for the topic(s) they are writing about • A writer's ability to see the world around them as full of possible topics and to collect ideas for future use
Focus	**What is this goal?** Controlling the piece so there is a clear, cohesive meaning related to a topic, an idea, a moment, and so on. **Look for:** • If the writer can articulate what their piece is about • If the details in the piece seem to connect back to one central idea, time period, topic, and so on

Continued on next page

GOAL	DESCRIPTION
Organization/ structure	**What is this goal?** Organizing the piece so that a reader is able to follow the story, argument, or information. **Look for:** • Clear beginning, middle, and end • Transitions between each part • If each part is well developed
Elaboration	**What is this goal?** Considering quantity, quality, and variety of details used in the piece. **Look for:** • How much detail is used to develop the piece • If the detail seems to fit with the meaning/focus • If the details are all one type (i.e., all action) or if there is a variety (i.e., action along with setting description, dialogue, character detail) • If the details fit with the genre of the piece
Word choice	**What is this goal?** Deciding what words help communicate a message or idea, or paint a picture in the reader's mind, or match the intended tone of the piece. **Look for:** • If the words are as precise and clear as they can be, in light of the focus • If the word choice matches the focus in terms of tone • If the word choice fits the genre • If repetition is intentional
Conventions: spelling	**What is this goal?** For younger children, using what they know to spell words as best they can, making good approximations, and taking risks to try to spell words. As children learn more spelling rules, using conventional spelling so others can read the piece. **Look for:** • What a writer does when attempting to spell a word • If the writer takes risks attempting words they may not know how to spell, using what they do know to spell as best they can • A pattern to the words that are misspelled • If the writer seems aware of spelling errors and makes attempts to correct them
Conventions: grammar and punctuation	**What is this goal?** Considering sentence variety, punctuation choices, and grammatical rules to communicate meaning and make the work readable. **Look for:** • If the writing is readable • If the writer appears to have made deliberate choices around grammar and punctuation (for rhythm, tone, flow, and so on)
Partnerships and clubs	**What is this goal?** Working in pairs or small groups to support and get support from other writers across the process. **Look for:** • How children work together at various parts of the process; is the work collaborative, supportive, and helpful

Now that you have a sense of what each goal is and what to look for, think about whether you agree with the order. Truthfully, there are times when you might make a decision that bucks this hierarchy, but in general it works. For example, you may decide to choose something relating to conventions for a student only once they've been able to choose topics they care about and worked to craft their writing with a clear meaning. Why? They are likely to be more invested in their piece and committed to getting the conventions clear so that others can read it. A student who needs support with elaboration and also engagement? You might choose engagement first—it can be beneficial to get into the flow of writing and enjoy it before offering a bunch of strategies for how to write more detailed pieces.

Of course, an additional layer to deciding whether a student needs support with any goal is to have an understanding of the expectations *within* the goal. For example, if I am thinking about the goal of focus, my expectations for a first grader writing a narrative would be that they would focus on a topic, but for a sixth grader, I would expect that focus to have some deeper message/theme in addition to the topic focus. That can be one place where skill progressions are useful.

Step 2: Use Skill Progressions to See Growth Opportunities Within Goals

Goals help to pinpoint a *category* of work that students will engage in to help them grow as writers. Within every goal, there are ways their work can be increasingly sophisticated. Becoming familiar with progressions can help you to:

• Build on students' strengths by noticing within the goal what students can currently do and looking ahead on the progression to what's next. This allows you to "build on students' knowledge, skills, and experiences . . . rather than chastise them for what they don't know" (Ladson-Billings 2009, 135).

Key Terms

The terms *goals, skills,* and *strategies* are used by educators in a variety of ways. Here's what I mean when I use them.

Goals: A large category. A goal is something that writers can work toward for several weeks, more or less. Goals can include multiple skills. One example of a goal is *elaboration*.

Skills: A skill is a proficiency, something a writer is able to do. Skills may be synonymous with *writing craft* or *techniques* or *moves* a writer makes. Examples of skills associated with elaboration are the ability to vary the types of detail, or being able to show and not tell.

Strategies: A strategy is a step-by-step how-to to help a writer work toward a skill and/or a goal. A strategy is not a single word or phrase; rather it is a series of steps, like a recipe. After the writer is skilled, the need to apply conscious attention to the strategy fades away. A strategy associated with elaboration is envisioning the character in your story, thinking about how that character feels, and then showing that feeling through describing their actions rather than stating the feeling.

- Choose appropriate strategies based on the next skill the student needs to practice.

- Monitor progress within a goal to choose next steps or to decide to move on to a new goal.

For example, during home quarantine in spring 2020 with restaurants closed, many friends and family members who'd avoided their kitchen suddenly took up cooking out of necessity. "Learning to cook better" includes a number of goals and skills: using knives safely and effectively, understanding leavening agents in baking, knowing how to balance flavor profiles, understanding how acids break down proteins, and more. Going from making toast and smearing it with Nutella to creating the perfect chocolate soufflé isn't something that will happen overnight. To perfect a soufflé, learning how to crack and separate eggs, beating eggs to a medium peak, heating milk without boiling or burning it, and noticing the perfect amount of rise and browning to know when the cooked custard is done are all skills the at-home cook needs to master. Recipes that practice one skill at a time—such as making a meringue cookie—might feel more accessible and less overwhelming. Accessibility leads to success. Success leads to a person continuing to put on an apron and get back into the kitchen for the next meal. (In case you're wondering, I do consider a chocolate dessert to be a perfectly acceptable "meal.")

When you become an expert on the substance of goals and skill progressions, you can guide your writers to the right focus at the right time to keep success and motivation high.

Skill Progressions Included in the Online Resources

Although there are ten goals in the hierarchy, some of the goals have more than one skill progression because of mode-specific information, hence the fifteen separate progressions. For example, the generating ideas skill progression applies to all modes and genres, but for the goal of elaboration, there are three separate progressions, one each for opinion, narrative, and informational writing. These progressions are informed by various standards including the Common Core, *Writing Pathways* (Calkins 2014), my study with Carl Anderson when he was writing his book *Assessing Writers* (Anderson 2005), and thinking I did when creating strategies and organizing them in increasing sophistication within each chapter of *The Writing Strategies Book* (Serravallo 2017).

Skill Progressions Within Standards and Grade-Level Expectations

A key for teaching and assuring your students grow as writers is having some sense of what growth looks like to build from where students are: that's what the skill progressions are all about. It's essential to be able to notice something a student does, and answer the question, what would it mean to do this even better?

One place to look to see how skills progress is standards; with standards, someone has already done some of the work for you to figure out how skills can or might progress. However, it's important to be cautious with standards, too. Standards and standardized assessments are often criticized for privileging one kind of discourse over another: it is often an academic English, "white language preferences" and a Eurocentric view of what makes for "good writing" that is emphasized, to the detriment and oppression of Black, Indigenous, and students of color, and emergent bilingual children (Inoue 2019; Kay 2020; Gannon 2020; Ascenzi-Moreno 2018; Hilliard 2002; Baker-Bell 2020). It's also important to keep in mind that every person develops at a different pace and that progression isn't always linear. Though we all walked and learned to talk at different ages, standards would have you believe that because you are nine years old and in third grade, you should be able to do X, Y, and Z. In truth, children are diverse in many ways—culturally, linguistically, neurologically—and each child's development will be unique.

And yet, you likely don't have a choice simply to ignore standards or standardized tests. As Souto-Manning and Martell write, "teachers experience

Composing with pictures	Organization/structure: poetry
Engagement	Elaboration: narrative
Generating ideas	Elaboration: informational
Focus/meaning	Elaboration: opinion
Organization/structure: narrative	Word choice
Organization/structure: informational	Spelling and letter formation
Organization/structure: opinion	Grammar and punctuation
Collaboration: partnerships and clubs	

a very real tension between getting students ready to take a high-stakes tests—which may or may not use culturally relevant material—and preparing them to think critically and engage in meaningful and culturally relevant learning" (2016, 11). So although it's wise to know and understand what children will be expected to do, and to support them while holding them to high expectations, we need to also make sure we appreciate the varied ways students compose and the different ways they may show growth and progress (Hammond 2015; Milner 2010; Howard, Milner-McCall, and Howard 2020).

All this is to say, it's important to be aware of the ways in which standards can be useful—while also being mindful of ways they can be harmful—while we work to remain flexible and responsive. Be open to seeing more than one way students can grow, recognize students' strengths and their brilliance outside of the narrowly defined set of skills named on the standards documents you use, and value the diverse ways that students might choose to compose, possibly outside of the genres or forms defined on the standards (Coppola 2019).

When you are using standards for help with understanding ways skills can progress, think about the consistent "categories" of work that are described, and notice the ways the work gets increasingly sophisticated through the grade levels. When you read the same standard across grades, in other words, you essentially get a skill progression.

For example, notice the progression of Standard 1 from grades 2–5 of the Common Core Standards (2010) on the next page. This standard deals with the organization of opinion writing. Highlighted is one particular skill: use of transition words. Notice how the skill increases in sophistication grade by grade in manageable, incremental steps.

As you look at the progression, it might make immediate sense to you. You might think,

GRADE 2	GRADE 3	GRADE 4	GRADE 5
Write opinion pieces in which they introduce the topic or book they are writing about, state an opinion, supply reasons that support the opinion, use linking words (e.g., *because, and, also*) to connect opinion and reasons, and provide a concluding statement or section.	Write opinion pieces on topics or texts, supporting a point of view with reasons. a. Introduce the topic or text they are writing about, state an opinion, and create an organizational structure that lists reasons. b. Provide reasons that support the opinion. c. Use linking words and phrases (e.g., *because, therefore, since, for example*) to connect opinion and reasons. d. Provide a concluding statement or section.	Write opinion pieces on topics or texts, supporting a point of view with reasons and information. a. Introduce a topic or text clearly, state an opinion, and create an organizational structure in which related ideas are grouped to support the writer's purpose. b. Provide reasons that are supported by facts and details. c. Link opinion and reasons using words and phrases (e.g., *for instance, in order to, in addition*). d. Provide a concluding statement or section related to the opinion presented.	Write opinion pieces on topics or texts, supporting a point of view with reasons and information. a. Introduce a topic or text clearly, state an opinion, and create an organizational structure in which ideas are logically grouped to support the writer's purpose. b. Provide logically ordered reasons that are supported by facts and details. c. Link opinion and reasons using words, phrases, and clauses (e.g., *consequently, specifically*). d. Provide a concluding statement or section related to the opinion presented.

"Yes, I can see how *and* is a less sophisticated transition word than *consequently*, not only because the word *consequently* is more complex, but also because the kinds of ideas linked might also be more complex. *And* means the two ideas are similar, *consequently* shows a cause and effect relationship." But there are likely times when *and* will do just fine, even when writing about ideas that are complex with complex sentences, and forcing *consequently* could feel artificial or make the writing cluttered. This is one of many examples of how progressions should be used as guides but don't always list "must haves" for writing to be considered more complex or sophisticated.

Whichever standards you use, check to see if they are organized the same way—the same skill is mentioned in every grade, and the work gets increasingly more complex. And also look at them critically to consider that the progression offered is *one way* the skill gets more complex *for some children*—but be open to other ways as well. The standards for opinion writing in the previous table, particularly, invite questions about whether a certain discourse is privileged and if there are not different ways students might grow when it comes to organizing and transitioning ideas and arguments in opinion writing.

You may also have professional texts that offer grade-specific advice that can be used as a guide. For example, *Writing Pathways* (Calkins 2014) offers detailed rubrics by grade level with work samples for three modes of writing: informational, opinion, and narrative. If you use a writing program or curricular resource, you may have grade-specific look-fors in the form of rubrics. Looking across rubrics from grade to grade or unit to unit might also help you see how expectations progress.

The fifteen skill progressions available in the online resources (see the box on pages 18–19 for more details) are offered for you to use as a guide—but not a rule of law—to notice strengths and envision ways for students to grow. Just remember, you can expect students to grow in ways *outside* of these linear progressions, too.

Download the skill-progression forms. See page xiii for instructions.

Word Choice

SKILL PROGRESSION

- Writer uses vague or repetitive language.
- Writer varies words to eliminate repetition.
- Writer uses words specific to the topic and/or genre.
- Student writes (and revises) with deliberate choice of words that match the genre's purpose (i.e., convince, entertain, surprise, describe, etc.). If there is repetition, it is purposeful.
- Writer attempts figurative language.
- Student writes (and revises) with deliberate choice of words, keeping audience and author's purpose in mind.
- Writer uses figurative language effectively to match author's purpose, mood, tone, and/or theme.

Using a Skill Progression to Identify Teaching Opportunities

Let's take a look at one of the fifteen skill progressions provided in the online resources. Notice how the work gets more sophisticated and complex from the beginning to end.

Now, take a look at one paragraph from a longer essay written by a fifth grader about the negative effects of technology on young people. In this particular paragraph, the writer offers evidence that technology can be addictive. If you look at the whole essay, it's clear she's been able to come up with a topic she's passionate about, she's stayed focused on her thesis statement, her piece is organized, and she has a good variety and quantity of details that match her thesis and reasons. But what about word choice?

Using the progression for word choice on page 22 as a lens, try to identify what the student is already able to do, what the next steps for her might be, and whether her word choices are grade/age-appropriate. Read the paragraph twice, the first time just to get a sense for what the writer is arguing, and the second time looking at the words the student chose. As you read, you might turn the language in the skill progression into questions. For example:

- Is the language varied or repetitive?

- Is the language vague or precise?

- Is the language used specific to the genre and topic?

- Does the word choice seem deliberate?

- Is there figurative language and if so, does it match purpose, mood, tone, or theme?

What do you notice?

Even though some people might think you can detach from technology whenever you want, the data shows that it is very addicting and you can be on it for longer then you intended. In the text "Negitive, Positive effects of excessive social media use on teens studied" the text says, "some doctors belive excessive social media should be recognized as an addiction, like an addiction to drugs or cigarettes." this is important because we keep kids away from drugs and alcohol but we don't keep them away from technology and social media but we should. Sometimes when a person is addicted to something it is the only thing they like or want and that is how some kids are behaving. In the video "Small talk Technology CBC' kids" One of the kids says "Yes I have an iPad and it is the only important thing in my life." This proves that kids are getting too addicted to their electronics when they should be playing outside and using their imaginations.

This paragraph comes from a longer essay about the effects of technology on children.

Here is my thinking:

Is the language varied or repetitive?	I notice the words *addicted, social media*, and *technology* are used often in this paragraph (and if they are used as much across the whole piece, it may be too repetitive and therefore something to work on).
Is the language vague or precise?	Precise, for the most part. For example, the use of the word *detach* is very clear and specific, and the use of the word *addicted* matches what the author is arguing for (that technology can have effects on people similar to that of drugs).
Is the language used specific to the genre and topic?	Phrases like *data show* and *this proves* are the sorts of phrases one would expect in a persuasive/opinion piece. Words like *technology* and *social media* match the topic.
Does the word choice seem deliberate?	I'm not sure about this one. To answer this question, I might need to interview the writer to ask about what decisions she made as she wrote, or any changes she made after a first draft.
Is there figurative language, and if so, does it match purpose, mood, tone, or theme?	While excessive social media use/addiction is compared to addictions to substances, this analogy is from another source, not from the author. This is an area where the student could use more work.

It makes sense to focus on word choice as a goal because of her (unintentional) repetitive language and because becoming comfortable with figurative language could help add more voice and craft to her writing. Working on strategies to deepen her word choice is something she seems ready to take on given the other strengths she has in this area.

As you're forming groups, it will be important to put kids together not just because they are working on the same goal, but often because they would benefit from the same strategy(ies) as well. For example, putting a group together for the broader goal of organization is less helpful than a group that will focus more specifically on transition words, or a different group that is working on the lead of their essays, or still another group that is working on making a plan for the overall structure. For the student whose essay paragraph we read earlier, other students who could benefit from eliminating accidental repetition, or who are ready to try figurative language, would make great additional members for the group.

Putting it Together: Using the Hierarchy and Skill Progressions to Identify a Goal and Skills

Let's look at another piece of writing. Read the five pages of a first grader's informational piece about swimming and reflect: What focus (goal) would benefit this writer?

Table of Contents

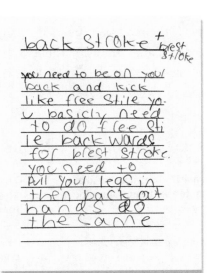

goggles   swim cap   baithing suit   floty

you need a swimm-cap it makes your hair stay dry also a baithing-siut! it also makes you dry! some goggles. they help you see under the water! cool!

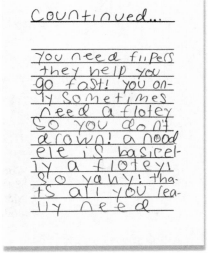

countinued...

you need flipers they help you go fast! you on-ly sometimes need a flotey so you don't drown! a nood ele is basicel-ly a floteyi so yahy! tha-ts all you rea-lly need

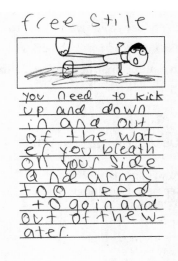

free stile

you need to kick up and down in and out of the wat-er you breath on your side and arms too need to goin and out of the w-ater.

back stroke + brest stroke

you need to be on your back and kick like free stile yo-u basicly need to do free sti-le back wards for brest stroke. you need to pull your legs in then back out hands do the same

In the charts that follow, I'll guide you through decision making using the hierarchy of goals as a guide. In the left-hand column you'll find the name of goals from the hierarchy and the look-fors you saw earlier on pages 15–16 phrased as questions. In the right-hand column, I've added "When would I choose this goal?" Because this is a first grader, I've narrowed the focus to the first few steps on each goal's skill progression; if the writer were an eighth grader, I'd be looking for evidence of everything on the progression.

Read the first goal, the look-fors, and the information in the right-hand column, then decide whether there is an opportunity to work within a goal, or if you want to explore the next goal. Much of what you see in the chart can be figured out by looking at the writing, though in some cases you may need to interview the writer or observe them in the act of writing.

GOAL AND LOOK-FORS	WHEN WOULD I CHOOSE THIS GOAL?
Composing with pictures—Does it seem like the writer is using pictures to plan out their piece and/or to illustrate after writing?	• The child does not use pictures yet. • Pictures don't match the words yet. • Pictures are not yet representational.

I notice the writer uses **pictures** to plan out the writing she'll do on that page. There is no picture on the page for backstroke and breaststroke because she chose paper without a box. I could encourage her to choose paper with space to use pictures to plan. I think she's able to do this (as evidenced from the drawing she did on the other pages), so I think this is worth a mention, but not something we'd need to focus on for a goal.

GOAL AND LOOK-FORS	WHEN WOULD I CHOOSE THIS GOAL?
Engagement—Does it seem like the writer is able to maintain focus and enjoy writing?	• There is a low volume of writing. • The child seems to lose energy for the writing/topic.
Generating ideas—Does it seem like this writer has come up with a topic that matters to her?	• The child has a difficult time coming up with ideas. • The child seems to write as if assigned, but doesn't feel invested in the idea.
Focus—Is the whole piece about one topic? Does the writer seem to have something they want to say about that topic?	• There isn't a clear topic. • Writer includes information that doesn't match the stated topic.

From observing her write, I noticed she is able to **come up with a topic** she cares about on her own, **stays engaged** for the entire writing period working on it, and the writing is all **focused** on one main topic (swimming). I do notice that what she planned to write and what she actually wrote are not the same. She planned a chapter on famous swimmers, another on lanes, and another on pool size that are missing from this book. Since she didn't finish the book, it may be that she could benefit from **engagement** strategies.

GOAL AND LOOK-FORS	WHEN WOULD I CHOOSE THIS GOAL?
Organization/structure—Is the information organized into clear subtopics, and do the facts within each subtopic fit on that page?	• There is not yet an introduction or a conclusion. • The piece is about one topic but information isn't organized into subtopics. • The piece could use transition words and phrases. • Facts are out of place (i.e., details about one subtopic are in a section about a different subtopic).

I notice a few opportunities to support her with **organization and structure**. I don't see that she has an understanding of introduction or conclusion yet (the opening line in her piece is "You need a swim cap," which doesn't introduce her overarching topic). She has some strengths in terms of her organization—her original plan organizes what she knows about swimming into subtopics. For those pages she did write, the information within each section does match the title on the page (i.e., the "What You Need" and "Freestyle" pages have relevant information). What's interesting is that she moves on to cram backstroke and breaststroke into one page (rather than separating them on their own, like freestyle) and doesn't mention butterfly. In her table of contents, she'd planned this to be the section on different strokes but then changed the titles on these pages. And then there are three more subtopics she'd planned to write about but didn't. I also don't see that she's using any transition words or phrases yet, either within a section or to move from section to section. This feels like a place where supporting her with strategies will help her writing, and also might even help her want to return to what she's started and work on it for a second day.

GOAL AND LOOK-FORS	WHEN WOULD I CHOOSE THIS GOAL?
Elaboration—Is there enough (quantity) detail, does the detail match the focus of each subtopic (quality), and does the writer use different types of detail (variety)?	• The details are all one type. • There isn't a lot of detail (just a sentence or two) in each section. • Some details don't fit with the topic or subtopics.
Word choice—Does the writer use words specific to the topic?	• Language is vague. • Language is unintentionally repetitive. • Words don't match the topic.

In terms of **elaboration**, she seems to have a lot of facts within each section and has even tried adding "partner facts" to say more. For example, she follows up "You need a swimming cap" with "It makes your hair stay dry." The "partner fact" gives more information. Her **word choice** seems precise. She uses words you'd expect to see in a book about swimming: *swim cap, goggles, stroke, breathe, freestyle*, and so on.

GOAL AND LOOK-FORS	WHEN WOULD I CHOOSE THIS GOAL?
Conventions: spelling—Does the writer spell conventionally correctly?	• The child doesn't take risks when spelling, using only words they are sure how to spell. • The child is unaware of spelling errors. • The child makes spelling errors that are unexpected, based on what they've learned in spelling/phonics/word study. (This child should spell correctly with consonants, blends, digraphs, short vowels, and VCe words, and should be able to record some sounds for every syllable in a multisyllabic word.)
Conventions: grammar and punctuation—Does the writer use punctuation and structure sentences in a way that makes it easy to read? What does the writer understand about capitalization?	• There aren't spaces between words. • The writing has no (or very little) ending punctuation. • The writer doesn't use capital letters.

She could use some support with **conventions**, especially ending punctuation and capitalization. She seems to record the sounds she hears and is using what she knows about spelling, and mostly spells words with short vowels and VCe patterns correctly, with a few exceptions (i.e., *strokes* is spelled *stroks*). Her other misspellings are more challenging multisyllabic words that I wouldn't expect her to be able to spell accurately yet because she hasn't yet learned double consonant rules or about vowel combinations like *ui* and *ou* (*different, famous, basically, suit, style, breast*) but it is a strength that she doesn't allow her inability to spell these words perfectly to keep her from using them, and she attempts using what she does know about spelling.

So, although she could use work in a few different areas, I would focus on the goal of **organization and structure** right now. Once we've worked on that for a while, we might spend a couple weeks on **elaboration** and then we'd move on to **conventions: grammar and punctuation**.

Grouping: Finding Patterns in the Class

All this talk about individual assessment in a book about small-group instruction? Why?

Well, for good reason. The most powerful small-group instruction will match the *individual*. Therefore, identifying clear goals and skills within those goals helps you keep the focus on each student as the unique writer they are, even when they are grouped with other writers for instruction. Most of the small-group types you'll be reading about in this book suggest pulling children together to work in a small group because they have a *common need*, so being able to identify the patterns easily will help you choose groups quickly and run the groups in a way where you can work efficiently and where students' needs are met.

Once you've done individual assessments, like the one you just practiced by looking at the swimming piece, you can then list student names, their goals, and other notes on an overview summary form, and look across the list to find patterns. If you create this chart in a spreadsheet, you could even color-code each row so the same goals are easy to spot: all those with engagement goals are green, those with organization goals are pink, and so on. In the chart on

NAME	GOAL	SKILLS, STRATEGIES, NOTES
James	Elaboration	Writing more, variety
Jessalyn	Organization	Introduction and conclusion
Nicholas	Elaboration	Writing more
Aniya	Generating ideas	Finding topics she's excited to write about
Stephen	Organization	Transitions, intro and conclusion
Matthew	Spelling	Vowel combinations
Sunita	Engagement	Monitoring distractions, attention
Obiazie	Word choice	Nouns, specificity
Shannon	Organization	Introduction and conclusion, sorting info into categories
Asia	Organization	Transitions
Dayana	Grammar	Complete sentences and ending punctuation
Noelle	Elaboration	Variety
Luz	Organization	Sorting information into categories
Julien	Grammar	Ending punctuation
Gabriella	Focus	Angling and focusing/narrowing topics
Tyquan	Elaboration	Variety
Aleah	Organization	Transitions
Nathaniel	Spelling	Multisyllabic words
Estefania	Focus	Angling and focusing/narrowing topics

Class-at-a-Glance: Informational Writing (All-About Books) October 2019

Download a blank, editable version of this form. See page xiii for instructions.

page 29, which students might work together in a group, if the group is focused on supporting students with the same strategy?

You could also use a checklist that includes specific information from skill progressions relevant for your group of students/grade level. The checklist that follows does not include every item from every progression, but it does capture the goals and skills that the students in one class are working on during this one unit.

Class-at-a-Glance: Fictional Narrative January 2019

NAME	GENERATING IDEAS: Topics they care about	FOCUS: Theme	FOCUS: Time/scene	FOCUS: Details match	ORGANIZATION: Introduction	ORGANIZATION: Rising action	ORGANIZATION: Conclusion	ORGANIZATION: Transitions	ELABORATION: Dialogue	ELABORATION: Setting	ELABORATION: Characterization	WORD CHOICE: Figurative language	WORD CHOICE: Verbs	GRAMMAR/PUNCTUATION: Vary sentences	GRAMMAR/PUNCTUATION: Quotes	GRAMMAR/PUNCTUATION: Paragraph	SPELLING: Catch mistakes	SPELLING: Spell multisyllabic words
Jessalyn										X	X							
Nicholas	X																	
Aniya					X					X								
Stephen		X																
Matthew														X	X			
Sunita															X	X		
Obiazie					X						X							
Shannon									X	X								
Asia							X	X										
Dayana							X	X										
Noelle																		X
Luz														X	X			
Julien															X	X		
Gabriella		X							X									
Tyquan	X																	
Aleah										X	X	X	X					
Nathaniel					X						X							
Estefania					X						X							

Download a blank, editable version of this form. See page xiii for instructions.

Whatever form you choose can serve as a living document as you work with students throughout a unit. As students learn new strategies and practice them, they will become independent and you'll want to move on to a new skill. After accomplishing all (or most) of the skills within a goal, it'll be time for a new goal. You could easily modify your class-at-a-glance form by highlighting new goals or skills to work on and checking off or dating the ones that the student has shown mastery for.

Step 3: Monitor Progress and Adjust as Needed

Although a child might be working on a goal for a while—several weeks, several lessons, several strategies—it's important to think of groups as being a temporary and flexible way to meet students' needs. They can be as temporary as just one day! This means that at the conclusion of each group, it can be helpful to stop and think, "Do I want to bring this same group back together to work on this same strategy, should I bring them together again to work on a new strategy they all need, or should I reshuffle the group and/or meet with them individually as a next step?" This way of thinking ensures that you are keeping an eye on the individuals within the group and always responding to individual needs.

In addition to creating a class-at-a-glance form to help you notice patterns in the class, it will also be helpful to take individual notes, even when students meet with you in a group. This will help you keep the focus on the individual learner, track their individual growth, and note what you might work on together next. In my notes, I try to record:

- what I worked on with the student during the lesson

- how they responded (Did they need a lot of support or were they fairly independent?)

- ideas for what's next (Was the strategy a good fit or should I try something different next time?).

Some will prefer to keep this information on a summary one-page chart, and others will want the space to write in more detail. One of the most important things to keep in mind when developing a note-taking system to monitor progress is that it works for you and you'll use it!

The solution I found for note taking after many years of trial and error is to use a two-pocket folder for each individual student: one side for reading and one for writing (see photo at the top of page 32). The folders are available to me when I work with individuals or groups in the classroom, and they are also portable and can travel with the student when they are working with another teacher (speech and language pathologist, interventionist, co-taught classrooms, etc.). Separate folders also allow you to easily spread out the notes on the table in front of you when you are working with several students at a time in small groups, while still keeping notes focused on each individual learner. On each side of the folder is a page where I write the goal we are working on

Reading skill-progression note-taking forms like the ones pictured are available as part of the online resources included with *A Teacher's Guide to Reading Conferences* (Serravallo 2019a).

at the top and where I have space to write strengths and next steps. Recently, I've been working with note-taking forms like the ones available in the online resources, which have skill progressions right on them. I find this helps to keep the focus on the goal and possible next steps and speeds up note taking since I can annotate the progression easily and don't need to write everything longhand. Of course, you could also use a digital cloud-based note-taking system such as Google Docs or Evernote to share notes amongst multiple adults and possibly even the student and/or the student's caregiver(s).

STRATEGY 5.8

Throughout this book you'll read about and watch videos of writing strategies coming to life in conferences and small-group instruction. You will see a green call-out to refer you to the strategy number in *The Writing Strategies Book* (Serravallo 2017) if you have that book and would like to read more about the strategy.

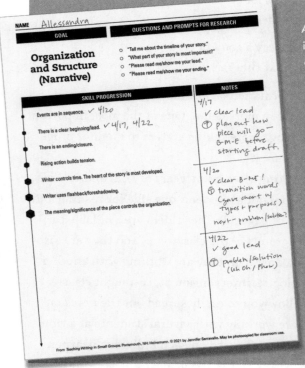

Allessandra, Marco, and Malik met in a small group with their teacher on April 22. She pulled them together because they all had the same goal (organization/structure) and also needed work on the same skill in the skill progression (crafting stories that focus on a problem and solution). Their teacher's notes, including some from the April 22nd small-group lesson where they learned the "Uh oh . . . UH OH . . . Phew" strategy, a strategy to help them plan out the plots focused on a problem that gets worse before it's solved (Serravallo 2017), are at left and right. Read across them to see what you notice. If

Step 4: Choose a Group Type

In addition to *what to teach*, you have options for *how to teach*. There are a variety of different types of small groups, each with their own purposes and structures, that can help you to meet students' needs and give them a just-right amount of support and independence to help them practice new strategies and incorporate them into their repertoire. In the chapters that follow, you'll read about each of these types of small groups and watch videos with students from grades K–8 filmed in classrooms and online during remote instruction. For now, read through the chart on page 34–35 for a brief overview of the variety of teacher-led small-group options. In addition to these seven small-group types, within many of the chapters you'll learn about one-on-one conferences you can practice or lean on to get ready to support students in groups, as well as student-led versions of some kinds of groups.

you were their teacher, what would be your next step for each of them?

The notes tell us that Marco got the hang of coming up with a problem to focus his story, but still needs help crafting a realistic solution. By the end of the small group, Malik also got the hang of the whole strategy and probably doesn't need follow-up (maybe just a quick check-in to see that what he learned in this group transferred to the next story he writes). Allessandra's notes just indicate the strategy, not that she mastered it, so she could use support again. It seems like Allessandra and Marco might come together for another small-group lesson to practice this strategy again, and Malik might get a check-in during a one-on-one conference next. No need to keep Malik in this group if he's already mastered the strategy!

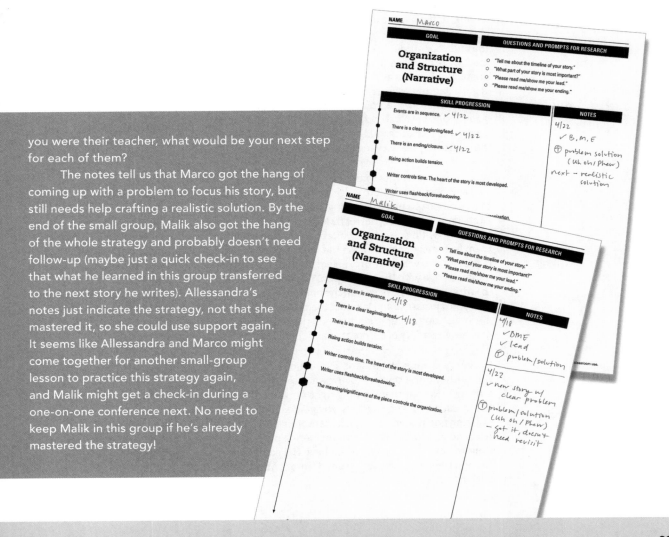

Small-Group Types at a Glance

CHAPTER NUMBER	GROUP TYPE	WHAT IS IT?	WHO IS IT FOR? WHY WOULD I CHOOSE IT?
4	Strategy lesson	Children are grouped based on the need for the same strategy. After a brief explanation of the strategy, each student practices on their own writing as the teacher provides individual coaching, feedback, and support. The lesson is laser-focused on just one strategy.	Any grade level Any goal
5	Guided writing	A few students come together to write, often on their own topics but sometimes on a shared topic, with heavy scaffolding and lots of prompting to help move them from sentence to sentence or word to word. Your role is to provide constant prompts and sentence starters. Although the focus of the group might be on one goal (i.e., adding elaboration), you might prompt for multiple strategies (i.e., ways to include action, setting, and dialogue into a narrative).	Grades pre-K–5 Most goals (likely not the best choice for generating ideas, focus, or partnerships)
6	Shared writing	You and your students collaboratively plan what you'll write or revise. Then, you scaffold the children's language and ideas as they compose verbally, negotiating and prompting along the way. Once students decide what to write, you do all the scribing and the result is one physical copy of the text. Since you'll teach children to integrate multiple strategies, the students in the group may have a variety of different goals.	Any grade level (though it will likely be used in lower-grade levels more often) Any goal except engagement and partnerships/clubs
7	Interactive writing	You and your students share the process of thinking of an idea and planning what to write, and you share the pen to co-compose a piece of writing. Although you involve all children in the group letter by letter and word by word (either by writing on a mini-whiteboard or by inviting them to, for example, "write in the sky" with their finger in the air), you will invite only select students to write on a shared page with the shared pen. You select students to write on the page based on their individual needs, so that you can assess and support them. Since the children are integrating multiple strategies in this group type, they may have a variety of different goals.	Grades pre-K-2 Focus most often on learning about writing process, how to get ideas in their heads onto the page, and how to orchestrate the many skills required for fluent writing (conventions)
8	Inquiry groups	In inquiry groups, the essential question is, "What has this author done that we might want to try in our own writing?" Rather than coming right out and answering the question for the children, you guide children in noticing and naming craft in a mentor or touchstone text and support children in considering purpose. Children in the group will often have the same goals, though they might benefit from different strategies within that goal.	Any grade level Any goal except engagement and partnerships/clubs

CHAPTER NUMBER	GROUP TYPE	WHAT IS IT?	WHO IS IT FOR? WHY WOULD I CHOOSE IT?
9	Reflection groups	Reflection empowers and motivates students to reflect on their work, celebrate what they've accomplished, and set goals for what to work on next. When you pull together a small group of students for the purpose of reflection, goal setting, and/or self-assessment, the students in the group will likely have something in common—such as a common goal—to make your coaching easier to manage.	Any grade level Any goals
10	Partner/ club small groups	Partnerships and clubs can be a valuable way for students to support one another across the process, but students will often need routines for working together productively as well as strategies for offering feedback to one another in respectful and helpful ways. When you confer with pairs or small groups, you coach them to have more productive and positive experiences working together. Each individual might have a different goal around process or genre since partnerships are set up irrespective of individual goals, and often last longer than the amount of time a student will be focused on a goal.	Any grade level Any goals (Though the focus is on partnerships and clubs, by helping the partnerships function well you are also supporting students with their other goals around writing process and quality.)

Tip

As you work to learn these different types of small groups, it can be helpful to focus on and practice one type at a time, for several weeks. Get comfortable with the feel and flow of the type of group and how to form it. As you become comfortable, try a new type to add it to your repertoire. Therefore, feel free to explore Chapters 4 through 10 in an order that matches your professional goals and the types of small groups that will be most helpful to your students right now.

TAKE IT TO YOUR
CLASSROOM

✓ **Practice, practice, practice.** Assessing student work using the hierarchy of goals and skill progressions will take some time at first, but with practice you will internalize the look-fors and questions and be able to spot teaching opportunities with greater speed and automaticity. Consider using the skill progressions provided in the online resources, your state or national standards, and/or assessment rubrics that come with the curriculum you use.

✓ **Create class overview tables or spreadsheets** to help you see patterns.

✓ **Take notes as you teach.** Try to record what you notice students are able to do now, what you taught, and what might be a next step. Try out the note-taking forms provided in the online resources, or create your own. Remember: What's most important is that your system works for you and you use it!

"Just because there are a small number of students in your charge at a given time doesn't automatically make them a suitable group for instruction; they need to have something in common."

UNDERSTANDING THE PRINCIPLES OF
Effective Guided Practice

In the previous chapter, you read about ways to identify goals for your writers, track their progress using skill progressions, and make decisions about how to group them for instruction. Though each small-group type you'll read about in Part II of this book has a slightly different purpose and structure, they all have some key research-based principles in common that will support students' growth and help them to become more independent with using the strategies you teach. Every one of the small-group types is an opportunity for you to:

- Respond to goals: teach students what they need.

- Offer clear, direct instruction: break down skills into strategies.

- Provide feedback as students try (and welcome feedback about your teaching from them).

- Invite students to do the work: give only as much support as each student needs.

Principle 1: Respond to Goals: Teach Students What They Need

When you use the hierarchy of goals and skill progressions to identify goals and to track student growth, you help ensure that what you practice in small groups is not work students can already do on their own (in which case the small group would be a waste of their time) and is not work that is overly challenging (in which case the small-group instruction could be frustrating). It's crucial that your instruction builds on students' strengths, knowledge, skills, and experiences (Ladson-Billings 2009). The instruction must help all children meet their full potential, communicate high expectations, and support them in achieving those high expectations (Howard, Milner-McCall, and Howard 2020; Milner 2010; Hammond 2015; Ritchart 2002; Means and Knapp 1991).

In the previous chapter, you also read about ways to view your class at a glance and to keep notes on progress to always make sure that your differentiated instruction is student centered, rooted in assessment, and dynamic, as Tomlinson advises (2001). In addition to *you* making sure that students are learning what they need to learn, it's crucial that students own their goals and their work; involving children in their own self-reflection and progress monitoring is inherently motivating and supports student agency (Hattie 2008).

Staying rooted in this principle of providing goal-focused, responsive instruction is important. Sometimes students are grouped for different reasons during a school day—an intervention specialist sees a group of four students at a certain time because of scheduling reasons, for example, or a teacher has more than half the class out at band practice and wants to make good use of the small group of remaining students. But remember, just because there are a small number of students in your charge at a given time doesn't automatically make them a suitable group for instruction; they need to have something in common. When you have four children with very different needs, rather than force a group lesson, it's often better to meet with them one-on-one and give them instruction that is responsive and builds on their strengths.

Principle 2: Offer Clear, Direct Instruction: Break Down Skills into Strategies

Identifying a clear goal, and even showing an example where the writer does what the children are aiming to do, often isn't enough for students to be able to do it in their own writing with independence. To use my cooking analogy from the previous chapter, it's like showing someone a photo of a chocolate ganache cake and asking them to make you one; to be successful, they need the ingredients list and the recipe. They need the *how-to*. In writing, it's the same thing: the goal is the *what* and the strategy is the *how-to*, the recipe.

Just like recipes, when we offer students *how-tos* in writing, they are most effective, doable, and clear when they are phrased in ways that break down skills into actionable, concrete steps. When we offer students strategies, we are empowering them with a procedure and knowledge that helps them with how they write rather than simply fixing up their current piece; as Calkins (1994) and Graves (1983) have said, it's important to teach the *writer,* not the *writing.*

STRATEGIES
1.16, 4.18,
6.4, 8.11

In some of the small groups you'll read about in Part II, the structure calls for beginning the lesson by naming the strategy clearly, then guiding children to practice it (i.e., strategy lessons). Other times, you'll read about getting children to practice the strategy (or strategies) and then naming it for them at the end to encourage transfer (i.e., guided writing). In others, you'll notice the suggestion to lead children through inquiry to help them discover writing craft, and then articulate what they noticed as concrete action steps as they are sent off to try it in their own writing (i.e., inquiry groups). But in every case, you'll see that strategies are an important ingredient in making the teaching explicit, the learning transferrable, and the skill doable.

GOAL	A SKILL, TECHNIQUE, OR EXAMPLE OF CRAFT	EXAMPLE OF A STRATEGY TO TEACH A WRITER *HOW*
Composing with pictures	Drawing representationally	"Touch what you want to draw. As you touch think, 'What is the shape? How big is it? How is it connected to another part I have drawn?' Once you have felt what you're going to draw, pick up your pencil and draw it."
Focus	Crafting a thesis statement	"Write a first draft of the arguments you want to make. Go back to the draft to underline possible lines, main points, or ideas that you think relate to the main point(s) you're trying to make. Try rewriting/rewording each several ways. Look back at your list and ask yourself, 'Which is the one that feels truest to what I'm trying to say? Which do I most care to prove?'"
Elaboration	Increasing quantity of detail (narrative)	"Think about what you want to write. Act out the first part. Sit and write down what you just acted out, using as much detail as you can. Act out the next part. Write it. After you finish, you can go back and act it all out again, to make sure everything you've acted shows up on your page."
Spelling	Spelling multisyllabic words	"Say the word you want to write. Clap the syllables. Listen to the first syllable. Think about what group of letters spell that first part. Say the word again, part by part. Write down the letters for the next syllable. Continue until the whole word is written."

Strategies make teaching explicit and skills doable.

Strategies are from The Writing Strategies Book *(Serravallo 2017).*

As crucial as strategies are when it comes to taking on new work, it's important to remember that they are *temporary scaffolds* and are meant to go underground in the writer's consciousness once the writer develops some independence and automaticity. There is a time when it is helpful to think, "Let me go back through my draft to notice the length of sentences I use, decide which sentences might be combined and which might be broken apart, and make sure I have a variety of sentence lengths to accomplish a rhythm." But eventually, we want the writer to be in touch with their voice and internalize sentence variety without applying so much conscious attention to it. It may be that you will coach and guide students in multiple small groups (or a combination of small groups and individual conferences) as they get comfortable with the strategy, but it's important always to be looking out for automaticity and transfer as signs to move on: to a new skill, strategy, or goal.

It's likely that you'll spend several weeks supporting students with a goal, and during that time you'll introduce several strategies. For example, see the following diagram:

STRATEGIES
3.24, 3.25,
3.27, 3.32

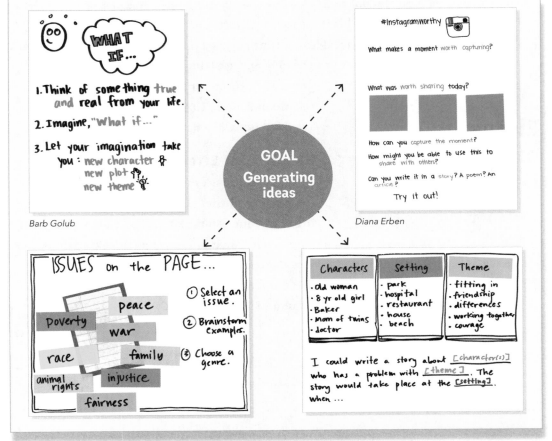

These charts summarize four strategies a writer might learn for generating ideas in narrative writing (*The Writing Strategies Book* [Serravallo 2017]).

A critical source of strategies is your own writing experience. When you are about to launch a study with your class focused on a particular genre of writing, or writing technique, have a go and create a piece of writing yourself. You'll be left with an exemplar you can use in your instruction, but it will also help you feel what it's like to write in that genre, notice aspects that are challenging, and "spy" on yourself as a writer to discover how you're doing what you're doing. When you notice what it is that you do, you can articulate it for your students.

Principle 3: Provide Feedback as Students Try (and Welcome Feedback About Your Teaching from Them)

Guided by student goals, you'll articulate clear strategies for students to help unpack for them *how* to do what you are suggesting they try. In every small-group lesson you'll read about in this book and watch in the video examples online, the emphasis is on student practice while the teacher guides, coaches, or offers feedback. In every lesson, this is *the most important part* and you will usually spend 75 percent or more of the total lesson time engaged in guided practice with feedback.

Why? "The very act of reviewing and applying feedback stimulates the growth of neurons and dendrites in the brain" (Hammond 2015, 102).

But not all feedback is created equal.

Elements of Effective Feedback

✓ Actionable and instructive

✓ Brief

✓ Specific

✓ Relevant

✓ Timely

✓ Generalizable

✓ Encouraging

Elements of Effective Feedback

First, the feedback must be **actionable and instructive**, rather than evaluative. You are aiming with your feedback to offer students the next step toward their goal or cues to help them progress (Hattie 2008). You're trying to help get the student from where they are to where they are aiming to be (Sadler 1989).

FEEDBACK THAT IS ACTIONABLE AND INSTRUCTIVE	FEEDBACK THAT IS NOT ACTIONABLE OR INSTRUCTIVE
"I notice as you read your sentence aloud, it helped you to find a place where a comma would help your reader. You heard it. Try to listen in the same way as you read the next sentence." "The main argument of your piece isn't clear. Try rephrasing your thesis statement a few times to see which sounds right."	"Great job!" "This would score a 3 on the rubric." "There are too many spelling errors."

Next, try to keep feedback **brief**. The more you talk, the less time and space students have to do the work. Too much teacher talk takes away student agency and can erode their confidence in your belief they can be successful. Give students space and wait time, and offer more support if necessary. Remember, productive struggle is a good thing (Hammond 2015). Children won't always generate what they want to say immediately; they need processing time and time to grapple with the strategy. It's a fine line, of course, between *productive struggle* and struggle that can feel frustrating. Keep an eye on a student's affect, and communicate your belief in them through your body language and your words. And there will be times when you need to say more to be clear, or to remind students of a strategy, or walk them through a few steps. If the moment calls for it, then by all means talk more. But if you can get away with saying less, do.

FEEDBACK THAT IS BRIEF	FEEDBACK THAT IS NOT BRIEF
"Reread to see if you can find a word that looks misspelled. Point under each word as you read."	"You want to make sure that all of the words are spelled correctly, so go back now through your whole piece and read each sentence and as you do that, see if there are any words that don't look right, or maybe look like they might not be spelled right. If you're not sure, you should go ahead and just circle it and you can always come back to it. For now, go back and reread to see what you think about each of the words in your piece. Did what I just said make sense?"

Aim to make the feedback **specific and relevant**, aligned to both the goal and strategy(ies) students are practicing during the lesson, and delivered one part at a time, so as not to overwhelm the writer (Hammond 2015). There will no doubt be other teaching opportunities that spring up during the lesson, or other things you notice in student writing that you may want to also address. Providing feedback only on the strategies aligned with your lesson objectives keeps the teaching focused and makes it more likely to stick. I often use words directly from the strategy in my feedback to ensure what I say to children during the guided practice aligns to what I told them we were practicing in the setup of the lesson. To help the feedback be as clear as it can be, when it makes sense, offer children clear "success criteria" in the form of a mentor text, exemplar piece of writing, or skill progression (Hattie and Clarke 2018).

FEEDBACK THAT IS SPECIFIC	FEEDBACK THAT IS NOT SPECIFIC
"Come up with three precise verbs that would make sense in the sentence in place of that word."	"Maybe there is more detail to include there?" "What are you going to do?"

Next, feedback needs to be **timely** (Hammond 2015). Provide feedback while the child is practicing, and offer prompts and questions that course-correct, nudge them along, or point out what they did well *in the moment*. The immediacy helps your feedback to be couched in the current learning context. When it's in the moment, you can also get feedback *from* students as they continue to practice, noticing what they do and don't understand. It turns out that research has found that children prefer immediate feedback, too (Hattie and Clarke 2018).

FEEDBACK THAT IS TIMELY	FEEDBACK THAT IS NOT TIMELY
"Go back and reread to listen for pauses where punctuation should go." "Right there! I heard a pause. Did you?" "Where does the ending punctuation go in the part you just read?"	"You just reread your entire story, and while you were reading, I heard about six or seven places where you could add some ending punctuation to help your reader. I'm going to send you back to your seat now to find where those six are."

Although it is specific to the strategy, feedback should be **generalizable** enough to apply across contexts, in other pieces of writing. It can be challenging to avoid getting into the details of the child's topic, the specifics of their sentence, the content of their piece. But the more applicable the feedback is, the more likely the student will be able to transfer and apply what you're saying the next time they are utilizing the same strategy.

FEEDBACK THAT IS GENERALIZABLE	FEEDBACK THAT IS NOT GENERALIZABLE
"What did your character say?" "Tell your reader *what* your character said and also *how* they said it."	"Right here in the story your character seems upset with her sister. I wonder what your character would say back to her that would show she's upset in this part?"

Perhaps most importantly: progress only happens when students are willing to receive feedback from their teacher. The content and tone of the feedback we offer children should communicate our honest belief that they are capable so that they have confidence to continue working. Feedback should be **encouraging** and delivered in a low-stress supportive environment where there is a strong relationship between teacher and student (Hammond 2015; Howard, Milner-McCall, and Howard 2020).

It's extremely important, though, that in an attempt to strike a positive tone, we don't soften our feedback or make it less clear or direct. In her book on culturally responsive teaching and neuroscience, Hammond (2015) shares research by Cohen and Steele (2002) who found that students of color taught by white teachers were more likely to receive feedback that was watered down or vague. Their theory is that teachers did this in a "misguided attempt to equalize a racial, linguistic, or socioeconomic power difference," but what actually ends up happening is that the student is unable to learn and grow from the feedback (Hammond 2015, 104). Hammond suggests that corrective feedback be given within a "sandwich" of positive feedback—this helps to convey faith in the student's ability to learn, while also being helpful and instructive.

FEEDBACK THAT IS ENCOURAGING AND HELPFUL	FEEDBACK THAT IS ENCOURAGING, BUT NOT HELPFUL
"In the beginning you used a balance of detail to bring your story to life. By the end of the story, you used all action. Remember, you know how to use dialogue, setting details, and show, not tell. Reread the second half to see what revisions you may want to make."	"You're growing so much as a writer and I can see that in the details you wrote about. You could always add more, you know, but only if you want to."

Feedback to Watch for and Ask for from Students

- ✅ Notice misconceptions; this tells you places where the teaching might need to be clearer.

- ✅ Pay attention to points during the lesson when children are engaged and when they seem bored; this gives you feedback on the pacing and length of your lessons, what you've chosen to teach, and/or a text you've chosen to teach with.

- ✅ Compare how students respond to one type of small group over another; this can give you some information about how students enjoy practicing new strategies.

- ✅ Notice when children put a strategy into practice immediately and without much support; this tells you they are ready to move on to more challenging work (either a new strategy or possibly a new goal).

- ✅ Notice when in the lesson your teaching seems to "click"; this tells you whether the student(s) learn best from watching you demonstrate or from their own practice/grappling with the strategy.

- ✅ Consider what students are looking at/to as they practice; this can give you information about how helpful your charts or demonstration texts are.

Feedback from Students

In small-group instruction, teachers learn from and receive feedback from students as well. In fact, this feedback is shown to be even more crucial to learning than feedback that teachers provide *to* students (Hattie and Clarke 2018).

Feedback *from* students is constant if you watch and listen, and in addition you can explicitly ask children to tell you how the lesson went for them and embrace what they have to tell you. When you invite feedback from students, "children see you are trying to get better at something [and] they begin to understand the labor and intentionality required to improve." In addition, when students are invited to give you feedback "it means that you value them . . . you are sending the message to all the children who witness that interaction that kids matter here" (Minor 2018, 88). See the sidebar at left for examples.

Types of Feedback

Different situations call for different types of feedback. For example, offering a student a *compliment* helps to reinforce something they are already doing. This type of prompt is very helpful when a student is independent with using a strategy and you want to celebrate their growth and make clear to them how what they are doing will be helpful to them in the future. A *redirection*, on the other hand, offers a high level of support for a student who may not be responding to other prompts and needs clear feedback on how what they are doing is different from the strategy they are trying to practice.

The table on the next page shows five common types of feedback. Notice the phrasing of the different types of prompts; consider how each example is a short sentence or phrase, not a paragraph of speech; and reflect on whether there is a prompt type that is more common or familiar for you. Are there any that you don't use routinely? If so, consider when they might be helpful to your students if you were to incorporate them into your feedback repertoire.

Prompt Types and Examples

TYPE	WHY?	EXAMPLES
Directive	To prompt the writer to do something specific	"Reread your first paragraph." "Say the word slowly." "Write that down!" "Listen for where the sentence should end."
Question	To prompt the writer to try something, to elicit information, or to get the writer to self-reflect	"What did you discover after you reread that paragraph?" "How can you figure out how to spell that word?" "What do you want to write down?" "Where should you put the ending punctuation?"
Redirection	To point out what the writer is doing and how what I'm prompting for is different	"You're looking across the whole essay. Just reread and focus on the first paragraph for now." "You're saying the word quickly. Try slowing it down to be able to hear each sound." "You've said a lot aloud. I think you're ready to write it now!" "I hear you pausing at the place where punctuation should go, but you're not hearing it yet. Go back and reread, a little slower this time."
Compliment	To reinforce something the writer does that they should continue doing; to celebrate progress toward a goal	"Your first paragraph is clear and sets your reader up to understand your opinion." "By saying the word slowly you heard each sound—and it's spelled correctly!" "I noticed you wrote without stopping and it really increased how much you were able to get down today." "When you read your writing aloud to yourself, you were able to hear your natural pauses, and now your punctuation will direct your reader to pause there, too."
Sentence starter	To nudge the writer by offering some language that they will often repeat, and then finish the sentence on their own	"I'm writing to you today because . . ." "Another reason . . ." "Later that day . . ."

Principle #4: Invite Students to Do the Work: Give Only as Much Support as Each Student Needs

Within each of the small-group lesson types in Part II, you can choose how much support you'll offer students. The high-support options are great for students who need it—either because of what you know about how they take on new concepts, or because they are new to a goal and you want to provide extra help with the first new strategy. But a common mistake is to start with the most support always, by default, and lessen support over time. This concept may have its roots in the gradual release of responsibility theory that suggests one way that children can learn—by viewing a model, then practicing with support, then eventually working on their own (Pearson and Gallagher 1983). And this does work well in many cases! But one of the beauties of a small-group lesson is that the teacher is there alongside students to guide them. In fact, in small-group or one-on-one settings, it's possible to forego the modeling and demonstration (the teacher-heavy support) and move right to the guided practice.

Keep in mind that often, the ones doing the most work are going to be the ones who are doing the learning. In other words, less (from the teacher) is often more. In many cases, I will tend toward *increasing support* as necessary versus providing a lot of scaffolding up front that then needs to be removed for children to be independent.

Following are some general guidelines about considerations for the amount of support based on group type, ways to vary support prior to student practice during the group lesson, and ways to vary the amount of support as students practice. The most important takeaway is to be mindful of the amount of support you offer to your learners and to help them be as independent as possible.

For example, choosing to demonstrate, giving an example, leading students through inquiry, simply naming a strategy, holding the pen versus sharing the pen—these are all decisions you can make. If you give a lot of help on Tuesday, for example, it'll be important to plan to repeat the lesson with less support later on. Or do the opposite: start with the least amount you

The amount of support that the **group type** lends itself to

The amount of upfront support **before students practice**

The amount of support **during the student practice** that you offer

You can think about the decisions around amount of support on three levels.

can get away with that allows the student to understand and approximate the strategy, and increase support in subsequent lessons only if and when a student shows they need it.

Amount of Support and Group Type

Each group type by design offers a certain level of support, though it's possible to increase or decrease support with your prompting and supporting *within* the group. As you read more about each group type in Part II, and watch the video examples of each, you can notice the balance of teacher talk and student talk and how much students do on their own versus how much support they need from the teacher. The following graphic will give you a sense of the amount of support each group type is designed to offer writers. You'll read about each type in Chapters 4 through 10 and will notice a "How Much Support?" feature that you can consult for more information. *Light* means more independence expected from children, and *heavy* means more prompting and feedback and possibly modeling or examples from the teacher.

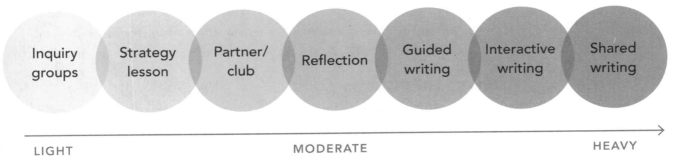

Each small-group type offers students a different level of support.

Amount of Support Before Students Practice

As you read earlier, it's best to spend the majority of time in a small-group lesson engaging children in guided practice—with students actively doing work and with the teacher offering prompts and feedback. There will be times, however, when you know students would benefit from extra support, up front, before they try. In these cases, inserting a short (approximately ninety seconds) demonstration, shared practice, or example/explanation would help to increase support within a structure that typically offers lower or moderate amounts of support. Again, include only one of these options if you feel you must—if it will really benefit the students in the group and set them up to be more immediately successful.

DEMONSTRATION

In a demonstration, you should *show* and *tell*. You can set up your demonstration by alerting students to what you are about to show them and explicitly state the strategy. It may sound something like this, "Writers, I'm going to show you how I think about the setting I've created for my historical fiction piece. I will check in with many of my senses, asking myself what I hear, feel, and see in that place, and then include details for each."

As you demonstrate, it's important to think aloud during *each step* rather than do the whole thing and point out at the end how it happened. This step-by-step demonstration helps writers to see *how* you were able to create the model you did, not just the end result or a great example. Sometimes, you might want to mess up on purpose; the intentional errors you make give you a chance to show how to troubleshoot in the moment and recover from mistakes.

Watch a 90-second demonstration.
See page xiii to access the online video.

Video 3.1

At the end of a demonstration, you can debrief what you did, articulating the strategy again. This repetition helps cement the learning for the writer and helps to make it more transferrable as you set them up to practice on their own.

SHARED PRACTICE

Watch a 90-second shared practice.
See page xiii to access the online video.

Video 3.2

Shared writing, guided writing, and interactive writing small-group types are designed as opportunities for students to engage in shared practice with you. But you can also bring shared practice as a method of teaching into other types of small groups, such as a strategy lesson. If you do this, you'd work together to create a very short (remember, aim to keep this at around ninety seconds) example of the kind of writing you'll have children practice on their own a few moments later. You can do all the scribing, or you can share the pen (or keyboard) with the students; either way, you'll play an active role in eliciting comments and suggestions from them. If and when students offer something that isn't a great example of what you're trying to model, you can shape their phrases and sentences so that what you end up with is a good example for everyone.

EXAMPLE AND EXPLANATION

Carl Anderson (2000) talks about the value of conferring "with a text under his arm," and many at the Teachers College Reading and Writing Project advocate for "conferring toolkits" that are collections of sample texts and other resources to have with you as you're working with children individually or in small groups. Finding a small handful of texts you can turn to again and again can speed up planning time and can increase confidence for any writing teacher ("Look! Jason Reynolds does this. You can, too!").

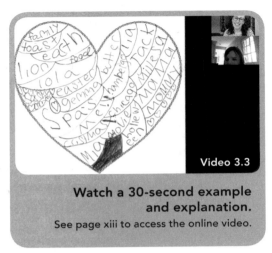

Video 3.3

Watch a 30-second example and explanation.
See page xiii to access the online video.

When you have a good example of a text to share with children, it'll also be important to point out what you want the children to notice and name clearly the strategy so that they can understand *how* the writer might have accomplished the technique.

INQUIRY

You can read more about inquiry groups—where the entire lesson time is spent in inquiry—in Chapter 8, but you can also use inquiry for a short period of time in another type of small group, such as a strategy lesson. When using inquiry, you guide children to notice and name a technique they see a writer has used. The writer whose work they may be studying could be a published writer, a piece of work you've created, or something another child has written. After noticing the technique or craft, you can offer students a strategy to help them to try it in their writing too.

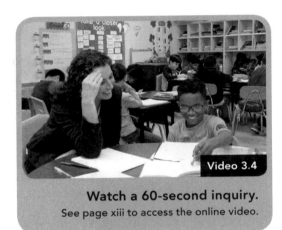

Video 3.4

Watch a 60-second inquiry.
See page xiii to access the online video.

Amount of Support as Students Practice

Earlier in this chapter, you read about feedback that you offer students being most effective when it's specific and relevant to the goal and strategy, timely, generalizable, and kind and encouraging. I also mentioned brevity because in general, I try to keep my talking to a minimum to allow for the maximum amount of time for students to practice. There are times, however, when you may need to give extra support in your prompts, or even offer a quick example for students who don't yet seem to be able to practice what you're asking of them. It's not necessarily a bad thing, it's just important that you're aware of how much support you're offering, and you have plans to offer less over time to encourage more independence.

I can remember times when I taught a small-group lesson and ended up doing most of the heavy lifting—offering a demonstration before the students had a chance to practice, talking a lot during their practice, maybe sometimes even doing some scribing for them. In almost all of those cases, I shouldn't have been surprised when little transferred back to the student's independent work after that first session. Just know that when you find yourself offering a lot of support—either because of the type of group, the amount of support you offer up front before they practice, or the amount of support during prompts—it is very likely that you will need to reteach the strategy again in a situation with less support.

As Hattie found in his research, "Simply placing students in small or more homogenous groups is not enough. For grouping to be maximally effective materials and teaching must be varied and made appropriately challenging to accommodate the needs of students at their different levels of ability" (2008, 95). As students practice within a group, it's important still to view them as individual learners and provide feedback for them as individuals. Although the group may have been set up with a certain level of support, you can vary the amount of support for each individual within the group through your feedback and coaching.

Strategy: Think of a list of questions your reader might have about your topic. Write each question on the top of a new page. Write an answer to each question in one, two, or three sentences.

STRATEGY 5.10

EXAMPLES OF PROMPTS OFFERING MORE SUPPORT (FOR CHILDREN WHO NEED MORE FROM THE TEACHER)	EXAMPLES OF PROMPTS OFFERING LESS SUPPORT (REQUIRING MORE INDEPENDENCE FROM THE STUDENT)
• "These two questions—do you think the answers belong on separate pages, or are they pretty similar and therefore should be combined?" • "It looks like you've got several very unique questions. Time to start answering them! Remember: one, two, or three sentences for each."	• "What questions do you have?" • "Write your question at the top of the page." • "Now go ahead and answer it."

Examples of Prompts with Varying Levels of Support to Support Students as They Practice

Strategy and prompts adapted from The Writing Strategies Book *(Serravallo 2017)*

TAKE IT TO YOUR
CLASSROOM

✓ Reflect on the four principles for effective small-group instruction—which truly are principles for effective *any kind* of instruction. How have these been instrumental in your whole-class, small-group, or one-to-one instruction so far? What shifts are you considering?

✓ Practice making some of your own strategies! You can start by doing a bit of writing yourself (even five minutes' worth will yield bunches of strategies), reflect on *how* you did what you did, and try to articulate some strategies as a series of steps. Practicing this on your own will help you to feel more comfortable doing it on the spot in front of students. If you have *The Writing Strategies Book,* you can look there for some more examples (Serravallo 2017).

✓ The next time you teach a lesson (any lesson), consider asking students to give you some feedback. Cornelius Minor (2018), for example, suggests telling children that you are trying to be clearer about *how* during your demonstration, not just showing an example, and inviting children to watch for it in your lesson and let you know how you did afterward.

✓ Consider audio or video recording a lesson and listen back for the feedback you offer students. Notice the length, type, and qualities of your prompts and consider them against the advice in this chapter about what makes for effective feedback.

✓ Listen back to an audio or video recording of a lesson and consider how much work or practice students are doing in the lesson, and how much work you do.

"As students practice within a group, it's important still to view them as individual learners and provide feedback to them as individuals."

PART II

Types of Small Groups

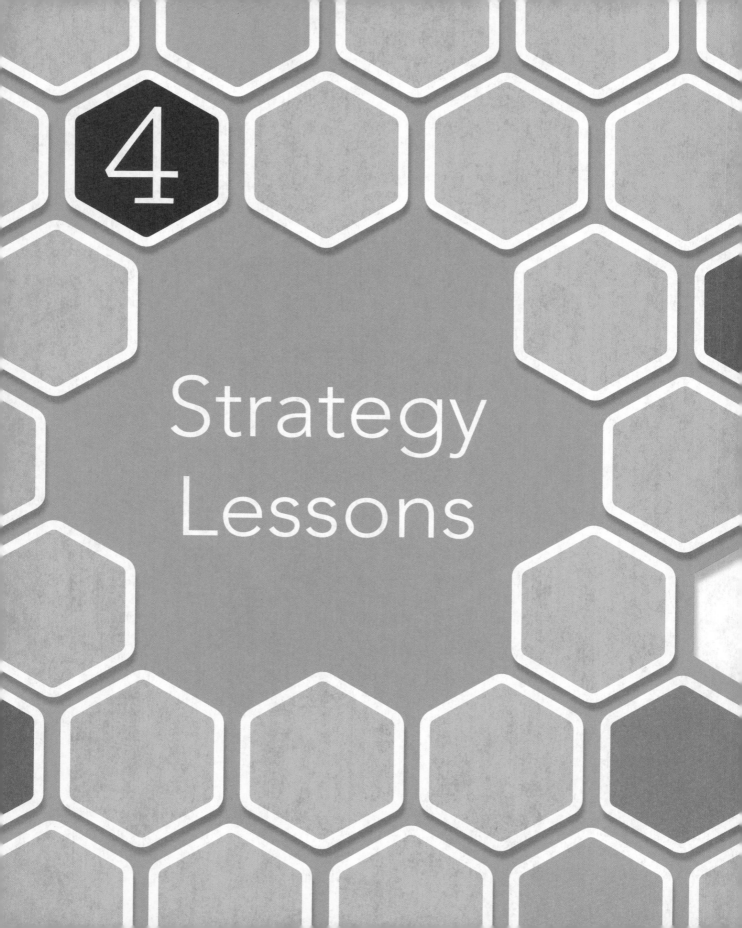

4

Strategy Lessons

Picture It: Seventh Graders Consider Word Choice

Three students settle at a table in the center of the classroom with laptops opened to their most recent historical fiction drafts. Mr. Cantor begins, "Writers, you're all working on a goal of considering your word choices. Today, I'm going to guide you to look for repetition in your draft. When we find a word that shows up again and again, you can highlight or underline it each time it appears, generate a list of synonyms for that word, then reread each sentence and consider if you'd like to make changes, swapping out a synonym for the repeated word."

STRATEGY 7.18

After a quick example with his demonstration piece, Mr. Cantor starts working with students one-on-one. They each have different topics and their own original stories, and the words they tend to repeat are unique to each of them. But the strategy will work for them all.

When Mr. Cantor leans over to Malaika, she tells him, "I see I've used *goes* twice already and it's only the second sentence." He tells her to do a "find all" search in her document to see if the word is repeated as much throughout, and sure enough *goes* lights up with a yellow highlight in almost every paragraph. "So do you remember your next step? Generate some synonyms."

After leaving her with that tip, he checks in with Jack. Jack seems to be repeating character names often, instead of using pronouns. He gives Jack a slight spin on this strategy, "So for you, it's not so much that you'll need to come up with synonyms. Instead, consider alternating the character's name and a pronoun, throughout the draft. Just make sure it's always clear who the pronoun refers to; you don't want your reader to get lost."

Mr. Cantor then moves his chair to the third writer. "I'm not finding any repetition," Rosie tells him. "Mind if I take a look?" he replies, and they look at the screen together. "Sometimes it can be overwhelming to scan the whole draft. Let's just compare sentence number 1 with number 2 and see if there is any overlap. Then we'll look at just one more after that. Sentence by sentence." Helping her study a smaller amount of text at a time allows Rosie to see the repetition. "*Went!* I use *went* a lot." "Yes, I see that too," he says, "I'm going to give you the same tip I taught Malaika—use your 'find all' tool now to see where else it appears, so you can get to the next step of the strategy and start generating synonyms and making revisions. Just make sure any synonym you select makes sense with the context of your sentence."

After the first round of coaching, Mr. Cantor checks back in quickly with each writer. Jack seems to be on a roll replacing proper names with pronouns. He reminds Jack to read the sentence and make sure it's clear who the pronoun refers to. Malaika has generated a list of five synonyms for *goes* and is already making appropriate replacements. When he comes back around to Rosie, he sees that she's struggling with the synonyms. "Another helpful tool in your word processing software is the thesaurus. Feel free to look up *went* there to see if it gives you some options for synonyms that will work in your piece," he offers, reminding her also to check to make sure any swap-outs make sense.

After about six minutes, all three writers are in process with the strategy. They haven't finished, and each writer may not have caught every instance of repetition, but Mr. Cantor is confident that they understand the strategy enough to continue on their own, so he sends them back to their regular work spots and gets ready to pull his next group.

When she entered her room she ~~went~~ (walked over) to her dresser to put on her favorite outfit: jeans with awesome patches on them, fancy lace lined shirt with the same color to match then she ~~went~~ (looked) in her closet to get her new black high tops then she put her hair in pigtails and ~~went~~ (walked) down the stairs and into the kitchen to eat a delicious breakfast of pancakes with syrup, butter on top, and a side of fruit salad! It tasted like happiness! Then she ~~went~~ (zoomed) out the door to her mom waiting in the car, excited and ready to start the fun filled day! Amy started to sing this song " i'm not going to school! I"m not going to school! Over and over for the full 45 minute drive to new york city.

When they got there Amy saw makenzie walking and ~~went~~ (ran) over to her " hi bestie!"

"hi bestie" makenzie replied.

Then Amy and makenzie ~~went~~ (got) into a conversation about who knows what, while Jon and Jen discussed things about their work project and how unfair the deadline was. Then something caught the corner of Amy's eye "look." she whispered to Makenzie their eyes widened and their mouths dropped as they looked up up up!

"Look at those towers!"makenzie and Amy said in unison

" that's where we work," Jon said, sounding proud

"well not in both only the one on the left" Jen added

Rosie's historical fiction draft with word choice revisions for *went*.

What Is a Strategy Lesson?

Strategy lessons are versatile: they are a great choice in any grade level, and they can be used to teach strategies to support just about any skill or goal. Strategy lessons even work well across subjects including reading, math, science, art—whatever!

In a strategy lesson, children are grouped because they would all benefit from instruction and guided practice around the same strategy. In essence, a strategy lesson is a coaching conference (see box below), but with two to four children at a time. Lessons often begin with a very short period of explicit teaching where you introduce a strategy and then explain, model, or involve children in inquiry or guided practice, followed by individualized coaching and feedback. During this coaching, each child works on their own piece—on their own paper or tablet or in their own notebook—as you support their practice one by one. Since the practice is individual and the lesson focus is about a strategy, you can easily manage supporting individual children who may be working on different topics (and in some cases even different genres!).

Work your way up to small-group strategy lessons by practicing coaching conferences first. A coaching conference is a one-on-one meeting between you and a student where you come prepared with a strategy to teach (or reteach) and offer the student strategy-focused feedback and support as they practice. It can be helpful for you to practice this type of one-on-one meeting before strategy lessons because you can give your undivided attention to the student and work on providing strategy-focused responsive feedback; later in a small group you'll be skipping around among two to four students. Watch an example of a coaching conference with a first grader working on organizing his nonfiction writing.

Video 4.1

See page xiii to access the online video.

conference

STRATEGY
5.14

Who is this for? When do I choose strategy lessons?

Grade levels	Goals
✓ Pre-K	✓ Composing with pictures
✓ K	✓ Engagement
✓ 1	✓ Generating ideas
✓ 2	✓ Focus
✓ 3	✓ Organization/structure
✓ 4	✓ Elaboration
✓ 5	✓ Word choice
✓ 6	✓ Conventions: spelling
✓ 7	✓ Conventions: grammar and punctuation
✓ 8	✓ Partnerships and clubs

Strategy lessons offer efficiency (why repeat yourself and do the same lesson with three children separately when you could teach them all at once?) while still offering individual support (through one-on-one coaching, as in a conference). The bulk of time in a strategy lesson is often spent on the guided, supported practice: you set children up to do the work, and you're there as a support, nudging them from approximation toward independence.

FAQ: But what if children have different topics? How can I manage them all in one small group?

The most exciting moments in my writing classroom have always been when children have a choice about the writing project(s) they are working on. Even when genre is assigned (i.e., we're in a unit of study learning how to write fictional short stories), students still have a choice of topic. And a few times a year, I pause genre studies to spend time helping children pursue their own independent writing projects, meaning I might have the thirty children in my class writing in fifteen different genres, all at once (Cruz 2004). There are many ways to pull children in groups around a common need, even when they are writing about different topics or in different genres. Here are two examples:

• You could convene a group to help students with a step of the writing process, for example, how to get ideas for a piece of writing. Many strategies apply well across genres. For example, walking to an important place—in reality or in your mind's eye—(such as the beach) can help you think of memories that happened there (to help a writer with personal narrative—"the time I built a sandcastle and a wave knocked it down"), think of topics that you could teach about the place (information writing—"all about different seashells you can find at the beach"), or consider ideas or opinions about the place (opinion writing—"we need to curb our plastic use to protect marine life") (Serravallo 2017).

STRATEGY 3.8

• You could convene a group to teach a strategy that aligns to a quality of good writing that transcends genre or topic, such as making good word choices. A strategy such as "Think about the audience you expect to read your piece and the words and phrases that will help them understand what you are trying to say. Make decisions about what words to keep, to cut, or to change" works no matter the genre or topic (Serravallo 2017).

STRATEGY 7.11

An added benefit of working with a group of writers, each with a different topic or writing in a different genre, is that it forces you, the writing teacher, to keep the focus on the *strategy* rather than the *child's specific piece of writing* or *specific topic*. This is also important in one-on-one conferences but can admittedly be more challenging to do. The conversation and coaching is then about *how* rather than *what*—for example, how to hear more sounds in a word and get those sounds down rather than just fixing the spellings of words. The power here is that the teaching is then stickier and more transferrable; you've helped the child learn something they will carry with them from piece to piece, rather than just making this one sentence in this one piece better.

Structure and Timing

Strategy lessons allow for the "I do, we do, and you do" of gradual release to all happen within a seven- to ten-minute span of time. The balance of time you spend showing and explaining the strategy versus having students practice can vary based on the needs of the students within the group, though in general I like to think of these groups as more like a conference (with the bulk of time spent on guided practice) rather than a minilesson (where often the bulk of time is spent demonstrating).

When I've written about strategy lessons in reading, I liken the role of the teacher during the guided practice/coaching portion of the lesson to a plate spinner (Serravallo 2010). At the start of the strategy lesson, you'll get all the plates spinning, and as you notice a plate wobble (in this case, a student who is in need of a prompt, redirection, or nudge), you'll work with that student one-on-one, briefly, until they are back "spinning" again, and you'll move on to another in the group. This coaching portion offers students in the group some breathing room to practice and approximate with you nearby, while one student at a time gets individualized attention.

HOW MUCH SUPPORT?

Strategy lessons are designed to be focused opportunities for a small group of students to practice one strategy. With most of the time spent with children independently practicing the strategy as the teacher moves from student to student, the amount of support in this type of small group is generally on the *light to moderate* side. It is possible to increase the amount of support by providing a demonstration or shared practice before setting children up to practice on their own writing. It's also possible to vary how much support you offer each student within the group, since the coaching you do will be individualized.

Strategy Lessons Go Like This:

1. **Connect:** Gather students with you at a spot on the floor or at a small table. Ask them to bring the writing they are currently working on. Tell them the focus of the lesson and why you've pulled them together.

2. **Teach:** Share a strategy. It can be helpful to jot the steps of the strategy down on a simple chart, piece of paper, or small whiteboard for easy reference. Depending on the support students need, you could give an explanation of the strategy, demonstrate it quickly in your own writing, show an example from a published piece or piece of student writing, or practice it quickly together by doing some shared writing. In most cases, try to keep this portion of the lesson to two minutes max.

3. **Coach:** This is the longest and most important part. As students practice the strategy on their own and in their own piece of writing, you will spend about thirty seconds with each one providing feedback, offering prompts, and lending support. To keep the lesson focused, be sure to coach students with trying only one strategy.

4. **Link:** Once students have had a chance to practice and have gotten some feedback (whether or not they've mastered the strategy) and time is up, repeat the strategy and send them off with a reminder of when and how/why to use the strategy. Many students will benefit from a visual reminder of what they've practiced to take with them—either a quick note they write themselves in their notebook or on a sticky note, or a mini-chart you've created for them.

Pause and Watch

Take a moment to pause your reading now and watch a video of a strategy lesson with a group of three fourth graders on the goal of "generating ideas."

Here are some important teaching moves to notice as you watch the lesson:

- ✓ The demonstration/example is super short so I can turn over the practice to the students quickly. I carry my notebook with me during small groups for quick reference and authentic modeling.

- ✓ I give wait time before offering suggestions, prompts, feedback, or nudges. I want to see what each student can do with a low amount of support before offering more.

See page xiii to access the online video.

- ✓ I tweak/modify the strategy in response to the student's practice. For example, when one student had an idea that started "I would always . . ." I suggested she focus on a "one time" story. I prompted another student to consider whether she'd come up with many ideas connected to one place or brainstorm many places and one or more ideas for each place.

- ✓ When David's idea is very close to his peer's idea, I don't insist that he come up with a completely original topic. Children can be inspired by and learn from their peers when they are sitting in close proximity during strategy lessons! Those who need this support can use it.

- ✓ After checking in briefly with each student, I circle back around for a second check. I spend a small amount of time coaching each student.

- ✓ I redirect students who are waiting on me to practice on their own. Their time is best spent if they are actively working with the strategy while I move from student to student to coach.

FAQ: What considerations should I make for writing process?

The truth is, there is no such thing as *the* writing process; most writers have *a* process that works for them, and that process varies from writer to writer. Although in general most spend some time planning before drafting and then spend time making changes, the amount of time writers spend on each, and microsteps within each, might vary from person to person. Some might go slowly through a draft, making sure each word is just right before moving on, revising while drafting. Others spill it all onto the page, knowing they'll spend a great deal of time with clean-up later. Others meticulously outline before trying to draft. Still others allow the act of writing to show them the way and use writing to discover what they want to say.

In the classroom, it is helpful and important to encourage children to work at their own pace through the process to maintain authenticity and engagement. When pulling them together for groups, you can consider the different kinds of writing work they are doing. For example, if the strategy you plan to teach really works best in revision (i.e., "Reread your draft to find words that repeat. Circle the words. Reread each sentence to consider if there is a more precise word that would fit."), then you'll want all of your writers to have a draft (or at least a portion of one). If you

Download your own copy of the graphic below. See page xiii for instructions.

This writing process shows one pathway from prewriting to finished piece. You may choose to hang an enlarged version of this (or something like it) in your classroom, and ask children to indicate where they are in their process by moving a clothespin, thumbtack, or sticky note as they go, to allow you to see the class at a glance. You could also give a copy to each student to keep in their writing folder.

choosing

developing
ideas
(tinker in
notebook)

generating
and collecting
ideas

rehearsing
(talk/sketch)

publishing

drafting

editing

revising

want to teach a strategy for editing, such as checking to ensure they used capital letters correctly, it can be jarring for a writer to think about conventions before they've gotten their ideas down.

Therefore, in addition to asking the essential question, "Do all the children I intend to pull for this group need the same strategy?" you will also want to make sure that they all are able to practice the strategy—meaning they are at a place in their writing process that will allow them to do so.

Another way to ensure that the teaching you'll offer in a small group is something that all the students can try, today, is to have children keep other in-progress writing and/or past pieces on-hand and also bring a notebook or folder with blank paper to the meeting. That way, if the strategy requires they have a finished draft, for example, they can always go back to a previous piece to practice and then try the strategy again on their current, in-process piece. Or, if the strategy helps them generate ideas to get started, the ideas they come up with during the small group can be used for their next piece of writing, and the strategy is one they can return to any time they find themselves stuck in the future. Having more writing to work with just gives them more options for practice, and after the group is over, students can go back to working on the piece they were in the midst of when you called them over.

Spin It: Sign-Up Groups: Students Choose the Strategy to Learn

Sometimes, a writer just knows what they need. Rather than waiting to be invited to join a strategy group, you could set up a sign-up in your classroom so children can volunteer to join a group that interests them. I started sign-up groups after reading about them in *Independent Writing* (Cruz 2004). It is every bit as empowering and motivating as Colleen describes to put children in charge of deciding what they want to learn and improve on, and the strategy lesson format makes doing them quick and easy. To do this, make the small-group options visible by posting them on a bulletin board, or if you're teaching online, you can create a shared document or whiteboard such as a Jamboard (see one example in Chapter 8, page 132). Students are invited to add their name throughout the day, and the teacher schedules the groups during writing time.

I love using these sign-up groups for any genre or at any point in the writing process. Here are a couple of examples of ways you might use them:

STRATEGIES
5.8, 5.27,
5.12, 5.31

- Imagine you teach a whole-class lesson offering a strategy to help students organize their writing by planning out a story using a story mountain. You could then offer sign-up groups that are variations or spins on that lesson, based on how the writer feels their story could go. For example, one group might offer a strategy for building tension. Another might offer a strategy for controlling time. Another might offer a masterclass in powerful endings (Serravallo 2017).

- During certain phases of the writing process, students will have very different needs. Take editing, for instance. As you work with children to polish their work, you might present them with a multi-item checklist including reminders about capitalization, spelling, complete sentences, and subject-verb agreement. Students might reflect using the checklist and rereading their drafts, thinking about which they can do on their own and which they might need a strategy and support for. Rather than you reading through all the drafts to put kids into groups (which would take a lot of planning time!), students can sign up right after the minilesson when you introduce the checklist, to get help with what they need that same day.

The idea of students self-selecting their groups is one that would also work with other small-group types. As you read about other types of small groups in the coming chapters, you can imagine spinning them into sign-up groups just like the strategy lessons described in this chapter.

Spin It: Student-Led Small Groups

As students work on their own goals and learn strategies over time, they will develop expertise. A great way to showcase their learning, empower them, and celebrate their knowledge is to give children the option to lead small-group lessons. Once students become regular members of strategy groups with you, they will start to internalize the simple, predictable structure enough that they can use it to teach their peers.

To get student-led small groups up and running in your classroom, you might decide to use the same sign-up sheet that you use for teacher-led student self-selected groups. Alternatively, you might notice a group of students who could use support from a strategy and invite a child to lead it: "Nakia, I know you just worked on learning different transition phrases to use during your essay writing, and there are a few students who could benefit from knowing what you know. Would you be up for teaching them the strategy I shared with you, and show them how you did it in your writing, and then help them try it in theirs?"

One of the things I notice from having watched many student-led strategy lessons over the years is that students will often rephrase things, or come up with analogies, that an adult may never have thought of, but that land perfectly with their same-age peers. I've often watched in awe thinking, "Wow. He taught that better than I did!" For example, in the video you'll watch in a bit, the student directs his peers to *anticipate counterarguments*, but uses his own language: "Say something back before they say it to you."

When students are new to leading small-group strategy lessons, you may choose to teach them how to write a lesson plan, as Jessica Lifschitz (2016) describes in her blog post "The Students Become the Teachers." They may also need support while teaching. I often sit in on the group, ready to support the student teaching like an instructional coach would support me as I teach. I might give them a subtle signal when it's time to stop talking and segue to giving the other students a chance to practice, or prompt the student teacher to speak up a bit, or hold up their writing so everyone in the group can see. Usually after one or two opportunities teaching with me as a coach, they are ready to lead groups without support. And of course, some children are natural-born teachers and don't need me at all! Once children are comfortable teaching and learning from one another, you'll multiply the number of teachers and experts students can go to for support with their writing, which makes the classroom feel even more like a writing community.

One important note and word of caution: if you are going to try student-led groups in your classroom, take care to have not only the students who are most expected to be teachers as the teachers. Make sure to give all writers, of varying abilities and differing strengths, a chance to shine as experts early and often.

Pause and Watch

Pause your reading and watch an example of a student-led small group.

This fifth grader is teaching a group of his peers how to anticipate counter-arguments and talk back to them in persuasive writing. As you watch the video, you might notice:

Video 4.3

See page xiii to access the online video.

✅ I'm sitting beside the student teacher. This is the first time he's led a small group so I want to support him. For example, I nudge him to offer his friends an example from his own writing after he's laid out steps, and I encourage him to peek at his friends' writing as they get started to see who he'll support first. (Also note: this was filmed during a lab site where I was teaching other teachers how to set children up to do this, so you'll hear and maybe see those other teachers in the background, too!)

✅ The student understands the structure of a small-group lesson because he's participated often with his teacher.

✅ The student is able to give clear strategy steps to his peers, which shows he's used to hearing strategies in steps from his teacher, and he's able to be metacognitive about how he's accomplished the work in his own piece.

✅ He puts things in his own words (i.e., "Say something before they say something back").

✅ He gives support to his peers in the form of coaching and positive feedback.

TAKE IT TO YOUR
CLASSROOM

✓ New to strategy lessons? Try coaching conferences first to get the feel for brief strategy-focused lessons and to practice giving pointed feedback to one writer.

✓ When you first try out strategy lessons, consider keeping your group small (two or three students). You'll find that it takes a little added concentration to move from student to student during the coaching phase and to take notes on each of them as individuals. The fewer you're working with, the less there is to juggle.

✓ Once strategy lessons are a common practice in your classroom, open up student choice with sign-up seminars, and invite students to be teachers with student-led small groups.

5

Guided Writing

Picture It:
Storytelling in Kindergarten

Mr. Nichols, a kindergarten teacher, recently launched a personal narrative unit of study. He's encouraging his students to think about true stories from their lives and write their stories with a clear beginning, middle, and end. He's been noticing a few children whose books sound less like stories and more like information texts. For example, a student who was writing about the beach wrote a three-page book: "At the beach there is sand. / At the beach you can swim. / I love the beach!" He thinks that doing some guided writing, focused on the idea that stories have a sequence of events and on the kinds of details that storytellers use (action, dialogue), could be just the nudge the writers need.

Mr. Nichols hands each child a three-page booklet and then begins. "Writers, we're going to work together today as you each write your own stories. Leah, you wrote a book about the pool. Can you think about *one time* you went to the pool? Gregory, you wrote about the beach. Can you think about *one time* you went to the beach? And Harper, you wrote about the park. Can you think about *one time* you went to the park?

When all three nod, ready, he continues, "OK, everyone think of the very first thing that happened that one time. Think about what you *did* that one time you were there. Can you picture it? Sketch it on your first page." As the children begin sketching, Mr. Nichols prompts them with language to make sure they are storytelling, even in their pictures, for example: "Who's in the story?" and "What are they doing?" He then has them say and sketch what will happen next, and after that, on their second and third pages.

STRATEGY
5.5

STRATEGY
5.2

Once they have a quick sketch, he nudges them to write a sentence. "Point to your picture. Now say out loud what you *did first*." After listening in to what each child says aloud and checking to make sure that they are writing an *action* (not *about* the topic), he tells them to quickly get the sentence down.

"Writers, characters in stories don't just do things. They also say things. Look back at your picture. Can you show what the character said? Add a speech bubble. And write the words that the character said in the speech bubble." As they do this, Mr. Nichols offers assistance—making a bubble larger to accommodate words. He redirects a child to write exactly the words the character said, not a summary of what the character said. He continues, "Now that you have it in your picture, you can add it to the story. Write 'I said . . .' and finish the sentence."

At the end of the few minutes together, each child has two sentences on their page—one action and one dialogue. For example, Lia wrote "My Dad throws squids for me to dive for" (action) and "Cannon ball!" (dialogue).

Mr. Nichols then directs the writers to look at their next page and say aloud what they will write. He reminds them to write one sentence about what the character *did* and one sentence about what the character *said*. He hands them each a Post-it with the key words *SAID* and *DID*. "Keep this to remember that as you write stories, you can add details about what the character said and what the character did!"

Notice that in this example lesson, Mr. Nichols guides the writers through much more than just two elaboration strategies. He also guides them through:

- understanding genre ("one time" versus "all about")
- setting up their three-page booklet with a plan
- visualizing the memory before drafting
- rehearsing verbally before writing
- ending one sentence and beginning another
- revising a picture by adding speech bubbles to remember what a character said
- referencing a sketch to add words on the page.

Yet, at the end of the lesson, he chooses to emphasize the two types of detail that he feels they are most ready to do independently.

FAQ: How do I prompt in ways that help all children in the group, even when they are writing about different topics?

Notice that the prompts used in the "Picture It" example are specific to strategies—focusing on one moment, writing sentences with action detail, adding dialogue—not specific to topic. The generalizability of these prompts is important because everyone in the group can use them at the same time, and also because as the students go back to work on the next page in their story, they will be able to use these prompts to remind them of how they did it. Here are some examples:

- "Think of the first thing you *did* when you were there."

- "What did you say?"

- "Write, 'I said . . .' "

- "Now write how you said it."

- "Write down the action."

- "Put a speech bubble in the picture to show what the character said."

- "Can you picture what's happening? Write what you did."

What Is Guided Writing?

In truth, all small-group writing instruction is *guided*. That's a primary reason for doing small-group instruction during writing time: to help guide writers to try out new techniques and strategies they aren't yet doing. What sets this type of small-group work apart from the others? I think of it as the amount of support offered to writers (a lot) and its structure (very controlled).

In a guided writing lesson, a few students come together to write, often on their own topics but sometimes on a shared topic, with heavy scaffolding and lots of prompting to help move them from sentence to sentence or word to word. Your role is to provide constant prompts and sentence starters to keep the writers in the group moving forward. Although the focus of the group might be on one goal (i.e., adding elaboration), you might prompt for multiple strategies (i.e., ways to include action, setting, and dialogue in a narrative).

Think of guided writing as just one step away from a demonstration. Your support is constant; like a parent holding on to the back of a bike running alongside the new rider, the riding wouldn't be possible if the parent weren't there. The parent prompts their child to keep their eyes forward, keep the handlebars straight, keep peddling—faster, faster!—and provides the necessary balance support with their hand. Most parents wouldn't want to spend every Saturday afternoon for months and months jogging bikeside; likewise, you shouldn't aim to use guided writing over and over for any student or group. Too much holding onto the bike and a rider might think, "I can't do it without my mom," just as a writer might learn dependence on you. But for a finite period of time, the high amount of support might be just what a bike rider (or writer) needs to get the feel of integrating *all* the aspects of the

Who is this for? When do I choose guided writing?

Grade levels	Goals
✓ Pre-K	✓ Composing with pictures
✓ K	✓ Engagement
✓ 1	Generating ideas
✓ 2	Focus
✓ 3	✓ Organization/structure
✓ 4	✓ Elaboration
✓ 5	✓ Word choice
6	✓ Conventions: spelling
7	✓ Conventions: grammar and punctuation
8	Partnerships and clubs

task—balancing, operating the pedals, angling the handlebars—and to begin to do them holistically and with automaticity.

Guided writing can be a nice balance to the more focused strategy practice students would get in a strategy lesson. Guided writing isn't a structure you'll choose for everyone, but when writers need extra support in a brand-new genre or to try on new skills around writing with increased volume, improving structure, or writing with more or a variety of elaboration, you can consider this group type. Guided writing can also be helpful for children learning to draw conventionally and compose with pictures, and even for children who need reminders to pay attention to writing conventions (such as capital letters and ending punctuation) as they write. You may choose these groups at times when your writers need to practice orchestrating a few strategies to get the hang of a new genre in order to work independently, or you may choose it when you've already taught a series of separate strategies and you want to guide children to draw from their repertoire and blend them.

Structure and Timing

In a guided writing lesson, sometimes students come prepared with a topic and genre, and other times you may provide it. When you provide the topic and genre, it is usually either to speed things along or to provide extra support (i.e., "We've all been learning about arguments for and against the continued production and use of plastic water bottles. Today we're going to work on crafting the plan for an essay to back up our opinions with evidence we've gathered"). When the students have chosen their own topics, they may have done so using a strategy they learned previously (i.e., "You all made a map of the heart and listed some of the people, places, and hobbies that are most important to you. Pick one and we'll draw a picture and practice labeling what we drew").

The bulk of the lesson involves lots of prompting to move the child from word to word or sentence to sentence (or in the case of drawing, line or shape to line or shape). While you plan ahead for the types of strategies and prompts that you'll be using, you are constantly watching the children during the lesson and responding with the prompts they need most. Most often, you can voice over to the whole group at once, rather than move from student to student as you might do in other types of groups, such as a strategy lesson. Keep an eye on students and watch for energy or fatigue, and stop the lesson when you feel they've had enough. In general, lessons tend to not be longer than ten minutes.

HOW MUCH SUPPORT?

In guided writing, each child is working on their own piece, but the teacher prompts them regularly by feeding them sentence starters and reminding them of strategies to use as they work. With this level of teacher involvement, this type of group typically offers writers a *heavy* amount of support, though if you prompt less frequently, you can lessen the amount of support.

Guided Writing Lessons Go Like This:

1. **Establish the topic and genre:** Welcome students to the group, make sure they are all set up with a topic—either one you provide or one they've chosen—and remind them of the kind of writing you'll be working on together. You might quickly show an example of the kind of writing they'll be making, or remind them of a text you shared previously that serves as a good example.

2. **Coach:** During the coaching phase, you'll support students as they each work on their own individual piece of writing. You can provide students with reminders and/or sentence starters that align to a variety of different strategies, not just one. You may have planned some of the ways you'll prompt during this portion, but you will also be constantly watching, assessing, and responding based on what you see. If there is a lot of struggle, you can slow down or narrow the scope of what you're prompting students to try. If they're getting it, you might go faster, give fewer prompts, or lift the level of what you're asking them to do. In this way, your coaching is both planned (or at least thought through ahead of time) *and* responsive.

3. **Link:** Before sending students off to work independently, you can repeat what you want them to remember most from what they were just guided to try with you. You'll focus on one (or maybe two) strategies you helped them to practice, not everything. Choose to call attention to what they are most likely to be able to replicate with independence as they continue on their own after a reminder; if you ran through a list of everything you practiced together, you run the risk of overwhelming their memory so that nothing sticks. The piece (or portion of a piece) they created with you will serve as their own self-created model when they begin to work alone, and you may ask them to annotate a portion with a sticky note, or jot a reminder of a strategy, to take with them as well.

Pause and Watch

Pause your reading to watch a video of a guided writing lesson with a group of four third graders whom I guide to write a persuasive letter.

Here are some important teaching moves to notice as you watch the lesson:

✓ The students in the group often don't produce a whole lot during writing time; I chose them for this group to help them gain confidence, get a lot of words on the page, and support them with the structure and detail in a persuasive letter.

✓ Most of the coaching I do in this lesson is in the form of sentence starters. This works well to coach children for structure and elaboration (the two main goals for the students in this group).

✓ During an in-person lesson, I would be able to peek at their papers. By videoconference, I ask them to hold papers up to the screen. With older writers who are fluent typists, I could also have each child open a Google Doc so I can monitor their writing as they work.

Video 5.1

See page xiii to access the online video.

STRATEGIES 5.16, 5.21, 5.30

✓ I tuck in examples occasionally if it seems that the students need them, but I don't feel the need to model all the time. Sometimes the sentence starter alone is enough to propel them into writing.

✓ I split students into breakout groups so they can share their writing privately (this is especially important for two of the children in the group who are working on building confidence) and also so the other students can focus and work in quiet. In person, I'd spread the children out a bit as they work so I can sit next to them and work with them one-on-one without our conversation disturbing the other writers.

✓ During one-on-one coaching, I support each student with individual needs. For example, I helped Ben clarify his opinion. I complimented Oliver on adding an explaining sentence. Even though we have a common goal in the group, one-on-one coaching can help each student get more precise feedback.

✓ I am trying to help the children get a lot down on the page, write in organized paragraphs, and add details (reasons, examples, or stories, and an "explaining sentence"). To stay focused on these, it means I need to let some things go (spelling, punctuation). I could convene the group again to support them with revision. As they work, I'm constantly assessing, and noting what next steps might be.

> Dear Sheena,
>
> I'm writing to you today because people need to stop littering. This is important to me because I see a lot of littering. Some people may think a little littering won't hurt but I know it will
>
> One reason you should change this littering is if you don't a lot of animals habitats will get destroyd. For example the polar Ice is dissapearing. This makes me relize littering will hurt animals too.
>
> Another reason you should change this is littering is affecting our life. For example littering pollutes the air which can then make us sick. This makes me relize littering is way worse because it is also affecting our lives.
>
> I hope you agree with me. If you do agree with me maybe you could make signs that say something along the lines of stop littering.
>
> Thanks,
> Penny

After the group ended, Penny finished the letter on her own. Notice how she was able to carry some of the craft she learned during the lesson to the portions she wrote independently.

TAKE IT TO YOUR
CLASSROOM

✓ Identify a few students who would benefit from lots of support to learn a new strategy or who need help learning to integrate a blend of strategies holistically.

✓ Clarify the goal(s) and strategies that will be most helpful to your specific group, based on what they show they can do and are ready for in their current independent work.

✓ To help you as you support the children in your group, brainstorm a list of prompts that are generalizable—that would work no matter what topic each student is choosing to write about, but that align to the strategies you'll be guiding them to use.

✓ Think about what your students can take away from your lesson to remind them of what they've learned when they are writing independently. It might be something you make ahead of time, something you make quickly on a sticky note while the children are writing during the lesson, or something that children jot down for themselves. Decide what is best for your group—quickest and stickiest!

"When you work to build relationships, your small groups will be more beneficial for you and your students. Also, working with children in small groups can help to strengthen relationships."

6

Shared
Writing

Picture It: Organizing Information into an Outline

A third-grade class has been learning about communities around the world, and each child has chosen several countries and cultural aspects—celebrations, food, school, clothing, and so on—to research. Today, they'll work on a shared piece before returning to their own independent pieces.

Ms. Wood starts by establishing a purpose for the group: "We've worked as a class to better understand cultures around the world. We've collected lots of information about celebrations to write a report, but we know that before we start writing, we need to get organized. I want to challenge you to go beyond what might be the first structure you think of, and instead we'll try out a few possibilities. Let's work together to come up with at least three outlines and decide which one makes the most sense."

STRATEGY 5.24

One student suggests organizing by whether the celebration has religious roots or not. Ms. Wood creates two possible chapters, one with each type of festival:

> Option #1
>
> 1. Religious — Holi, Diwali, Festa Junina
>
> 2. Not Religious — Chinese New Year Lantern Festival Carnival Chale Wote Pana fest

Ms. Wood and her group discuss that the chapters might feel a little unbalanced, and one would be much longer than the other. She asks, "How else might we organize the information to get more chapters, each with a more equal amount of information?"

One student suggests organizing by country. Ms. Wood asks them to say what chapter one would be, and what sorts of information they'd include. Then, what Chapter 2 would be, and so on until they've created the following possible outline. Ms. Wood scribes as the group dictates:

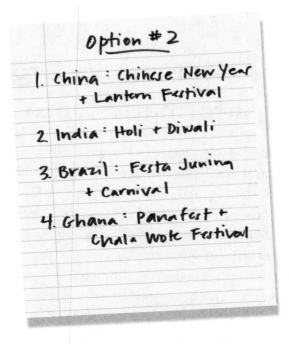

"That might be the best way to organize it. But before we commit, can anyone think of one other way the information might be organized into an outline?" She gives pairs within the group a chance to turn and talk, and one partnership suggests that since they have so many facts, they could really make each festival or celebration its own chapter. Ms. Wood helps them to outline that option, and they come up with this:

Option # 3

1. Chinese New Year
2. Lantern Festival
3. Holi
4. Diwali
5. Festa Junina
6. Carnival
7. Pana fest
8. Chula Wate Festival

She next asks them to share which way they'd organize the book if they were writing it—two of the four choose the second way, and two choose the third way. They spend a little time discussing why: What's the effect on the reader? How much information would be in each chapter based on how it's organized?

Ms. Wood concludes the lesson by highlighting some key takeaways: "Writers, as you go back to your seats to review your information, I want you to remember that there are many ways to organize information into parts, sections, or chapters. Like we did here, try to make fewer chapters and then more chapters, try to put different information together, rearranging until you have the outline that fits best with how your reader will understand what you have to say and based on how much information you have. With informational writing, and really with any kind of writing, it is often worth taking a little time getting the structure right before you begin to draft."

What Is Shared Writing?

Shared writing is a great choice when you aim to offer students a lot of support, almost as much as a demonstration, but in an interactive, engaging way. If the group will be working on a new piece during the shared writing lesson, the text is planned collaboratively with you and the students in the group. Then, you scaffold the children's language and ideas as the text is being composed verbally, negotiating and co-composing. Once the text has been decided on, you do all the scribing (Routman 2005; Fountas and Pinnell 2017). It is also possible to have a revision or editing focus in shared writing. In this case, the group works together to read a previously written piece, you scaffold students' language and ideas as they decide what to change, and you record all the changes. Either way, you hold the pen the entire time so the writing (and session) moves quickly, and you end up with a strong exemplar piece that students can return to as a model to study as they work on their own writing. A text can be short and written in one sitting, or longer and written over the course of several sittings.

Shared writing differs from demonstration because you involve students in planning and co-composing; in demonstration, *you* do the planning and composing, thinking aloud for students who are observing as you compose.

Shared writing is also different from interactive writing (which you'll read about in Chapter 7), though they are often confused—which makes sense, because they're sort of like cousins! The big difference is that in interactive writing, students help with the *scribing*—you invite them to use a shared pen and write on a shared page. You also typically address different types of goals in the two types of groups. In interactive writing, you focus more on emergent writing skills and behaviors, spelling, and letter formation; in shared writing, you address

Shared Writing Benefits: Upper Elementary

I choose small-group shared writing most often in the primary classroom, although there are clear benefits in certain cases in upper elementary as well:

- Because language is structured during the shared composition, you can work on language goals alongside writing goals for emergent bilingual students.

- For students who are going to be writing a new genre for the first time, using shared writing to take them through the whole process of composing, possibly over a series of small-group lessons, can serve as a strong foundation for them before they write their own pieces

- Since the text is co-composed, it can be a more engaging option than modeling for students as they watch.

goals that are broader in scope and more varied. In both interactive and shared writing, there is a great deal of conversation and collaboration between you and students.

During a small-group shared writing lesson, you'll plan the lesson focus(es) in advance based on what the children need most; it's likely there will be *several* skill and/or process objectives each time. For example, you might decide to help a group with how to come up with ideas, coach them through planning out a story, and tuck in strategies for how to offer more details as you write.

Any time you choose shared writing, it is to "raise the standard of what's possible" by being an "expert for your group of apprentices" (Routman 2005, 84). In that way, you play an important role by not only accepting whatever students suggest to write down, but to help shape their language so it's more sophisticated, readable, elaborated, organized, or whatever you're trying to help them learn to do with guidance.

Who is this for? When do I choose shared writing?

Grade levels	Goals
✓ Pre-K	✓ Composing with pictures
✓ K	Engagement
✓ 1	✓ Generating ideas
✓ 2	✓ Focus
✓ 3	✓ Organization/structure
✓ 4	✓ Elaboration
✓ 5	✓ Word choice
6	✓ Conventions: spelling
7	✓ Conventions: grammar and punctuation
8	Partnerships and clubs

Structure and Timing

Shared writing is highly interactive the entire time, with conversation between you and your students, and among the students, throughout the entire ten-or-so-minute lesson. During the lesson, you begin by establishing a purpose and then guide the children in orally composing (when writing a new text), or rereading critically (when editing or revising a previously written text). You elicit from students what to write or what to change; children contribute the words you'll scribe onto the page. It's important to keep a lively pace to keep engagement high.

During shared writing, you hold the pen and act as scribe, and also prompt children to elicit their suggestions for what to write. You guide them through the process, sometimes even suggesting a topic. This group type provides students with a *heavy* amount of support.

Small-Group Shared Writing Lessons Go Like This:

1. **Plan and Rehearse:** Set a purpose for the writing the group will do together and invite children to turn and talk to their partner or as a group to plan and compose out loud, or if they are returning to a piece to revise or edit, you might reread the piece together and discuss what sorts of changes need to be made.

2. **Write (Draft, Revise, or Edit) Together:** After rehearsing aloud, elicit from children what they'd like you to write down—either new sentences or changes to a previous draft. Pause often to support children as they orchestrate the strategies you want them to practice; what you guide students to think about or try will depend on the goals you have for the group. During this phase, look for opportunities for all children to participate, and help all students to be successful and shine.

3. **Reread:** Often, and throughout the process, involve children in a shared reading of what they've written. This will help cement the important habit of checking what has been written down to make sure it makes sense and to help prompt children to remember what they wanted to write next.

4. **Link and Transfer:** After composing the text, articulate the main takeaways that you hope students will remember and bring with them as they work on their own writing. Following the lesson, you may make photocopies of the text you created together, to serve as a reminder and model as they compose their own.

Pause and Watch

Video 6.1

See page xiii to access the online video.

Pause your reading now to watch a video of a shared writing lesson with a small group of three first graders.

Here are some important teaching moves to notice as you watch the lesson:

✓ Before writing, we talk a little together. Oral rehearsal can be helpful for children, and it is something I encourage children to do when they are writing pieces independently, too. Therefore, the process we follow during shared writing can be a process they follow when they are writing on their own.

✓ In this lesson, I emphasize how writers get ideas for poetry (in this case, from a photo start) and elaborate (by prompting them to use their senses). As I write, I add line breaks and shorten their longer sentences into poem-like lines. I don't call out what I am doing in this lesson, but I will later in a subsequent lesson when we focus on line breaks and stanzas.

✓ For the most part, I accept what they offer in the way of details as long as they make sense.

STRATEGIES
3.4, 6.13

✓ Typically, I reiterate the main strategies I coached the children to practice at the end of the lesson. These three seemed "done" so I skipped it, but I'd plan to start with calling out the strategies the next time we meet.

✓ When I invite the children to reread with me, they are quiet. In person, I always insist that they read chorally, but over video conference it can be hard to sync our voices, so choral reading is next to impossible.

Valuing All Students' Contributions and Efforts

Since shared writing gives us a chance to mentor students into more sophisticated work than they are able to do on their own, there are times when children will feel some stretching and productive struggle.

Learning can often happen during these moments of temporary discomfort, as long as children feel safe and supported and that their own language and culture is respected (Hammond 2015). One of the moves you'll use during shared writing is to redirect students. When you do, it's important to be careful about your language to offer support coupled with respect and caring.

Instead of…

Try…

"No, we don't say it like that. Who knows the right way to say it?"

"Oh, yes. Let me say it back to make sure I'm understanding."

"Yes, that's one way to say it. Another way I've heard it is . . . Which should we write?"

"Who has a better idea?"

"Let's collect a few ideas and decide together which one we want to keep."

"That's too long."

"Let's practice saying that a couple of ways until we get the language as clear as we can."

"If you were to use just one sentence to make that point, how would you say it?"

"Hm. That doesn't make sense to me."

"Tell me more so I can understand and get your idea down."

"You're not using your resources."

"Check the room and see what might help you figure out the spelling of that word."

Another potential challenge is eliciting ideas from quieter or more reluctant students. Setting all students up to know you're there for them and that their approximations are valued will help them speak up during the lesson. Try phrases like:

- "You said you don't know, but if you did know, what would you say?" (Hat tip to Ellin Keene!)

- "Give it a try. I'm here to help if you need it."

- "How about if I give you the first couple of words in the sentence to get you started, and you finish it."

- "Everyone turn and talk with your partner and be ready to share out the idea your partner had."

- "We're just throwing out ideas now. We'll keep some, and tuck some away to use later."

- "Part of rehearsing aloud is trying out ideas we might and might not end up keeping. Just try and see what comes out!"

- "Tell me your idea, and I'll suggest a few ways you might want to say it. You pick the one that sounds best to you."

- "You've got this. I know you do."

- "I see the risks you're taking—that's how learning happens!"

FAQ: What kinds of writing work well for shared writing?

Any kind of writing that exists in the world! Although you may often choose to do shared writing aligned to your writing unit to give students extra practice with the process, structure, and craft, consider using small-group shared writing across curricular areas and to help children craft writing that they won't be formally studying during writing time. For example, consider:

- writing explanatory texts in math to recount the steps students took to solve a problem

- writing a lab report to capture the materials, steps, and outcomes of a class or small-group science experiment

- creating a slideshow presentation to teach about a social studies topic students are studying

- writing letters of gratitude to classroom helpers, school staff members, or families

- creating signs to hang in the hallways, bathrooms, or cafeteria to address a community issue

- keeping a class reading notebook, building a variety of ways to respond to reading throughout the year

- writing short reviews or recommendations about favorite books, and posting them on a board near the classroom library for others to review as they browse for new books

- responding to current events with short letters to the editor

- crafting a poem to respond to a weather event the class witnessed together

- writing lyrics to a song that will be set to music and practiced during music class

- writing a welcome sign for the classroom door before back to school night

- creating classroom charts together to remember strategies, procedures for partner time, ways to use writing materials, routines for unpacking upon arrival, and so on

- composing a list of agreements for working together during club time.

TAKE IT TO YOUR
CLASSROOM

- ✓ Identify a group of students who could use a clear model—either of a new genre, of a step of a process (i.e., revision, editing), or of a skill (i.e., elaboration).

- ✓ Consider what you might write (or revise) together to help support the students with the goal(s) they are working on.

- ✓ As you teach the small-group lesson, keep an eye on the time. You can always return to the piece to work on it later if you aren't finished and time is up or the energy in the group seems low.

- ✓ Consider making a duplicate of whatever you create in the small group for each child to keep with them to serve as a model or mentor text for them to return to as they work on their own pieces.

"The feedback we receive from students about our teaching is crucial to be able to revise, adapt, pivot, and change, to positively impact learning outcomes."

7

Interactive Writing

Picture It: Spelling Practice in First Grade

It's fall in a first-grade classroom in Columbus, Ohio. Ms. Wright identifies four children who are each working on a spelling goal. After studying their written work, the beginning-of-the-year high-frequency word assessment, and the spelling inventory, she's jotted notes about the specific spelling features each child is working on and some high-frequency words (HFW) that she would like them to learn to spell with automaticity.

Asa	Kamal	Lulu	Zahira
• Long vowels • HFW: *the*	• Blends and digraphs • HFW: *of, are*	• Endings (*-s, -ed, -ing*) • HFW: *the, in, to*	• Blends • Digraphs • HFW: *in, the, are*

Once Mrs. Wright groups children based on a goal (in this case, spelling) and identifies what they need to practice (in this case, short vowels, blends and digraphs, endings, and some high-frequency words), she then needs to make sure that the message they'll be writing together offers the children a chance to practice some or all of what they need to work on.

Mrs. Wright offers an authentic purpose for today's lesson: a sign to go in the cafeteria that would remind children what to do with their waste when they are finished eating. In their school, garbage, recycling, and compost are separated into different containers, but not all children have gotten the hang of it yet.

Before pulling the group together, Mrs. Wright brainstormed some ways the sign might go. Using *trash* instead of *garbage* would allow Kamal and Zahira to practice the /tr/ and /sh/, and for Asa to practice short *a*. *Compost* allows Asa to also practice the long *o* in the second syllable and for Kamal and Zahira to practice hearing the two letters that spell the /st/ at the end of the word. When Mrs. Wright thought about the high-frequency words, she realized that full sentences would work best, so she considered three small separate signs to hang above each bin that say: "Put the trash in here" and "Put the compost in here" and "Put the recycling in here." In these sentences, the children can practice *the* and *in*, and the word *recycling* would allow Lulu to work on the *-ing* ending.

PROMPTS THAT HELP WITH HEARING SOUNDS AND RECORDING LETTERS	PROMPTS THAT HELP WITH WRITING HIGH-FREQUENCY WORDS
• "Let's say the word slowly." • "What sound do you hear at the beginning of the word?" • "What letter(s) make that sound?" • "Say just the last sound." • "Two letters make that sound." • "Do you know another word that starts the same way? How does that word start?" • "Write it on your own whiteboard as __ writes it up here." • "Let's reread what we wrote. Did we get the sounds down that we heard?"	• "Where could we look in the room to find that word?" • "Let's all say the letters of the word as __ comes up to write it." • "How many letters are in that word?" • "Write that word in the sky as __ writes it." • "Write the word with your finger on your knee as __ writes it on the page." • "We know that word! It's on the word wall." • "Let's check what we wrote. [Spell aloud] Does that spell __?"

No matter what spelling features you're teaching or what words you want children to practice writing, the above chart offers some predictable prompts you can use to have children practice the spelling strategies they'll need.

The group begins with Mrs. Wright reminding the children of the problem they are having in the cafeteria. She asks them to turn and talk about what signs they could make to help children remember to throw their lunch waste in the right containers.

After they turn and talk, Mrs. Wright suggests the three separate signs. "Let's start with the first one: *Put the trash in here.*" She writes the word *put* quickly, then asks the children for help with *the*. "Where can we look to find that word?" she says. All the children point to the word wall, and she has them all spell it aloud, and invites Lulu up to the sign to write it while the others chant "*T-H-E! T-H-E!*" She then has them reread what they've written so far and asks them to say the word *trash* slowly. She asks Kamal to write the *tr*, Asa to write the *a*, and Zahira to write the *sh*. The lesson continues with Mrs. Wright writing the portions of the text that don't offer good opportunities for the students to practice what they need, or that are too challenging (such as the *cycl-* in the word *recycling*) for what they are working on now.

STRATEGIES
8.2, 8.10

The portions of text that the students worked on aligned to their individual needs. This finished piece now serves as a model to all of them, and the guided experience gives them confidence to apply these same strategies when they write independently.

Put the compost in here.

Put the trash in here.

Put the recycling in here.

What Is Interactive Writing?

During interactive writing, a teacher guides young children who are learning about writing process to orchestrate the many skills required for fluent writing, from idea to draft to revision. In this type of small group, you and your students share the process of thinking of an idea and planning what to write, and you share the pen to co-compose a piece of writing. Although you guide *all* children in the group letter by letter and word by word (either by asking them to, for example, write on a mini-whiteboard or "write in the sky" with their finger in the air), you will invite *select* children (based on their individual needs) to write on a shared page with the shared pen as you assess and support them.

Interactive writing is different from *shared* writing (see Chapter 6) where children and teacher work together to compose a text but the teacher does all

the writing, holding the pen the entire time. And it is different from *guided* writing (see Chapter 5) where students work on their own piece while a teacher guides and coaches them sentence by sentence or part by part.

Interactive writing is common in (mostly) kindergarten classrooms as a whole-class structure, but it also works well as a small-group structure for targeting specific skills and goals within and beyond kindergarten. An additional benefit of a small group is that students are much more actively involved in the writing than they can be during whole-class instruction, which increases their engagement and helps the teaching to stick (McCarrier, Pinnell, and Fountas 2000). Once students begin writing with more fluency and independence, you'll likely shift away from interactive writing to more shared writing, strategy lessons, or guided writing to support their growth (Fountas and Pinnell 2017).

Since the group members will be co-composing the piece, they need a shared, authentic purpose for writing and common background experiences so they can all be involved, just as with shared writing (see Chapter 6, pages 98–99). They may, for example, work together to write a letter to the principal or a classroom visitor, an alternate ending for a story they all read together, a shopping list of art supplies for the classroom, the procedure for a science experiment, a sign to hang somewhere in the school or classroom, a pattern book they will reread during reading time, or a classroom chart to serve as a reminder of something they've learned.

In addition to what the group will write about, you will also need to know the specific writing skills and strategies you want students to practice and make sure that the writing experience lends itself to that practice. As McCarrier, Pinnell, and Fountas (2000) write, "In the planning process, you are deliberately trying to elicit a particular kind of writing, and you have in mind some of the characteristics of text that you want the children to learn" (85). So, for example, hearing the beginning and ending sounds in words is possible in any kind of text

Who is this for? When do I choose interactive writing?

Grade levels	Goals
✓ Pre-K	✓ Composing with pictures
✓ K	Engagement
✓ 1	✓ Generating ideas
✓ 2	✓ Focus
3	✓ Organization/structure
4	✓ Elaboration
5	Word choice
6	✓ Conventions: spelling
7	✓ Conventions: grammar and punctuation
8	Partnerships and clubs

you plan to write, but if your goal is to help children consider when to use capital and lowercase letters, a type of writing that would include proper names, rather than a shopping list, would be a good choice. Students work through the writing process during an interactive writing lesson, therefore they practice all aspects of composition. However, I am most likely to choose this lesson type when I want to focus on the goals in the chart on page 107.

Notice the variations in handwriting: the teacher, Kristine Mraz, wrote some, and each of the children in the group contributed to different parts, based on what they needed to practice.

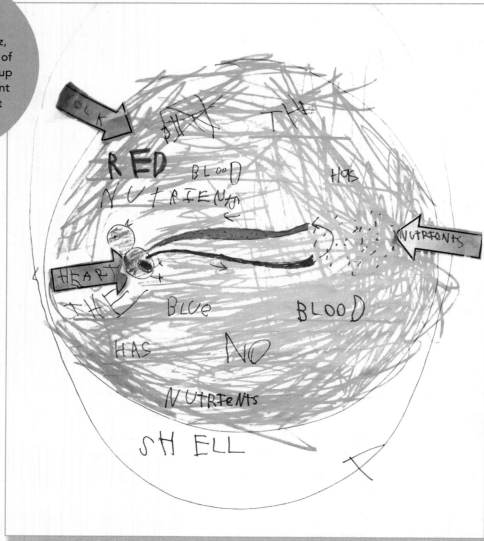

Structure and Timing

Students are heavily involved in composing the text in interactive writing lessons, and you guide them by going slowly and being deliberate, voicing over what a writer needs to think and do to get the letters, words, and ideas onto the page. With frequent pausing and prompting, it can feel like the pacing drags, or that something that seemed like it would take no time at all to co-compose with the children takes much longer than expected. The ideal length of time for a small-group interactive writing session is no more than ten minutes. In this amount of time, it's often possible to plan and write a short list (like a shopping list of items to buy for the gardening project), one sign (such as a sign for the hallway asking passersby to speak in whispers), or one page of a book (with an illustration and single sentence). If you want to write a longer piece, consider composing it over several separate interactive writing sessions.

HOW MUCH SUPPORT?

During interactive writing, you will help children with the process of coming up with a topic, planning what to write, and then composing on a word-by-word level. This group type usually provides writers with a *heavy* amount of support. To lessen the support, you could involve children in doing more of the writing, and you could prompt less often.

Small-Group Interactive Writing Lessons Go Like This:

1. **Plan and Rehearse Verbally:** Set a purpose for the writing the group will do together (i.e., "We are about to get a new class pet and I need help writing a list to take with me to the pet store"). Invite children to turn and talk to a partner about what they will write on the page. Of course, you will have planned ahead for some of the writing features you need to include for students to practice, so you may need to negotiate between what they say during the turn-and-talk and what you'll write together.

2. **Draft Together:** After rehearsing aloud, guide children through getting the message down on the page. Pause often to support children in doing the work of orchestrating multiple strategies (i.e., "I know that's a word we know how to write. Can someone find it for us on the word wall?") and invite children to come up to share the pen (i.e., "Sanjay, will you please come up and write the first letter of the word *the*? And it's the first word of our sentence so it'll need to be what kind of letter, everyone?") and involve all children in practicing (i.e., "Let's everyone write a capital *T* in the air with your pointer finger as Sanjay writes it on the page").

3. **Reread:** Often, and throughout the process, involve children in a shared reading of what they've written (i.e., "Let's reread what we have so far. *The party is going* . . . what was the next word we wanted to write?"). Rereading teaches children an important habit—to make sure what they've written makes sense—and it also prompts them to remember what they wanted to write next.

4. **Link and Transfer:** After composing the text, articulate the main takeaways that you hope students will remember and take with them as they work on their own writing.

FAQ: Does everything in the finished piece from an interactive writing lesson need to be correct?

In short, yes. This is a unique feature of this type of group, and there are some reasons why. First, the piece of writing that you make together can then serve as a model for when children work on their own pieces independently. If you guide children to write with you and allow errors (like a capital letter in the middle of the word, a missing space between words, a misspelled word) to stand, children may erroneously think that what is on the page is correct (their teacher co-wrote it with them after all), and then they might copy errors into their own writing.

Allowing errors to stand in a piece of interactive writing is also a missed teaching opportunity. Making errors as we write is something we all do; learning how to catch ourselves and revise as we go is an important skill that we can guide children with during these lessons. When a child makes an error during an interactive writing lesson, use a sticky note or "oops tape" to cover up the error, explain the correction that needs to be made, and support them in correcting it.

It is crucial that you balance interactive writing lessons with other opportunities throughout the day for children to write independently, and in those instances, they should be encouraged to use their strategies and what they know and spell and write as best they can. If they try to write conventionally perfectly at age five, it is likely they will be taking no risks and you will end up with pieces that have only high-frequency words and CVC words. Writing with meaning at the forefront means they will need to take some risks and write words with approximated spellings to say what they want to say.

Pause and Watch

Video 7.1

See page xiii to access the online video.

STRATEGIES
9.1, 8.5, 8.2,
8.3, 8.4,
8.7

Pause your reading to watch a video of an interactive writing lesson with a group of six kindergarteners.

Here are some important teaching moves to notice as you watch the lesson:

✅ I begin the lesson by giving a purpose for writing that's connected to a shared experience, so all children can participate in composing the text.

✅ Children in the group are working on the concept of one-to-one matching, so we count the words, and then I write blank spaces on the page with spaces.

✅ I stop frequently to emphasize key points connected to the goals of children in the group:

- Hearing sounds and connecting sounds to letters: I involve them in saying words slowly. I am careful to make sure they respond to the prompt "What letter makes that sound?" with a letter name, and "What sound do you hear?" with a sound. We work on digraphs and blends as well such as /th/ and /cl/.

- Capital versus lowercase letters: we check the alphabet chart to note differences between capital and uppercase letters, describe the differences in letter formation.

- Using resources: we check the word wall for high-frequency words.

✅ When there are parts of words that children would not be able to spell accurately (because they haven't yet learned the word or because they wouldn't be able to sound it out), or an entire word, I write that part of the word quickly.

✅ As one child comes up to write on the page, I invite the rest of the class to "write in the sky" and "write on the carpet."

✓ When a child makes an error, I help the child correct it. What's on the page should be conventionally correct (see the FAQ about this on page 111). If your goal is to support children with making spelling approximations, getting words down the best they can to utilize their full range of vocabulary—an incredibly important goal for young writers—you might teach them to do this in a strategy lesson (Chapter 4).

✓ We reread often to check that what we've written makes sense and to remember what we'll write next.

✓ At the end of the lesson, I remind them of what we practiced over and over again (hearing the sounds in words, using the word wall) that they should take back to their own writing.

FAQ: What assessments might help me best understand what to highlight in interactive writing?

The most powerful interactive writing lessons are ones that guide children to practice strategies and behaviors that support your goal(s) for them, and that they are on the cusp of being able to use independently. Through your guidance and with opportunities for repetition, students leave the group ready to transfer what they've learned to independent writing. But what are the strategies and behaviors that children are on the cusp of knowing, using, and being able to do? How do you know? Here are some places to focus your assessment:

A Writing Sample. Any writing that a child has produced on their own offers you insights into which skills and strategies they are using without support and what would be most helpful to support their growth. As you study an independent writing sample, consider what conventions of language, or aspects of the writing process, might help them most.

> Look at all there is to learn from a single writing sample.

Work on adding spaces between words

Work on capital vs. lowercase letters

"It was in pieces and it wasn't green."

and

letter formation Z vs. S

work on adding ending punctuation to a complete sentence.

Kidwatching. Watch students during independent writing time to determine if they need help coming up with a topic or getting started. As they write, notice if they are using the resources in the room (word wall, charts, alphabet card or strip). Listen in as they write to see if they are saying words slowly to hear the sounds to help them write.

Phonics. Whatever phonics assessments you use, and the scope-and-sequence of the program you are following to support your students, can help you to pinpoint specific phonics principles to practice during the lesson. Interactive writing does not replace explicit systematic phonics instruction, but it can serve as a helpful reinforcement to teach children to apply what they are learning as they write.

Spelling. Spelling inventories like the one included in *Words Their Way* are not about recalling specific memorized words, but are rather to help you to pinpoint which spelling *features* students still need support learning (Bear et al. 2012). Interactive writing does not replace spelling instruction, but it can serve as a helpful reinforcement to teach children to apply what they are learning "on-the-run" as they write.

Concepts About Print. Marie Clay's (2017) assessment looks at which print concepts (such as the concept of letter versus word, the function of ending punctuation, or left-to-right directionality) students know and what they still need to practice. Although CAP is designed as a reading assessment, interactive writing is a chance to make reading and writing connections, and the information gleaned in this assessment can identify areas for reinforcement in interactive writing lessons.

Letter Identification. Letter ID assessments will help you figure out which letter names and which letter sounds students are coming to know with automaticity. The letters and/or sounds that students are still working to learn would be great ones to highlight during a small-group interactive writing lesson.

High-Frequency Word Identification. Knowing the spelling of some high-frequency words and being able to write them with automaticity helps students to write fluently. A high-frequency word identification assessment will help you to know which words children can read automatically, but you will still need to check to see if they can write these words with the same automaticity. Learning to write words is one "way of knowing" that word; depending on the student and depending on the word, at times the ability to write the word will come first, and other times recognition of the word in print will come first. Interactive writing can be a great place to make the reading-writing connection for children.

Although this child knows all but five letter names, there are many opportunities in interactive writing to teach her the sounds that correlate to each letter.

Name:_____ Date: _____

	Name of Letter	Sound of Letter
A	✓	" eh "
W	✓	" duh "
P	✓	✓
K	✓	✓
F	L	/i/
Z	✓	✓
U	no reply	/k/
J	no reply	✓
O	✓	uh
H	no reply	no reply
B	✓	✓
M	✓	✓
Q	✓	"juh"
L	✓	"e/"
Y	✓	/k/
C	✓	/s/
I	✓	" uh "
X	✓	✓
S	✓	✓
N	m/sc	/m/
D·	✓	✓
T	✓	/f/
V	no reply	/z/
R	✓	"uh"
G	✓	"juh"
E	✓	/y/

Spin It: Reading-Writing Connections: Using Interactive Writing to Create Texts That Will Support Students in Independent Reading

Reading and writing are inextricably linked, and the more we can make meaningful links between them for children, the more quickly they learn! For example, when learning to read, pattern books offer children a chance to see high-frequency words repeated until they become automatically recognized sight words. Writing the same words again and again helps children spell them with more automaticity.

A small group of children worked together to create a patterned alphabet book including images of their favorite animals, which they enjoy re-reading during reading time.

One idea for a reading and writing connection is to write pieces with children, make copies of them, and then add them to the collection of texts they read and reread during independent reading time. For example, you might create a simple five-page story that follows a pattern with a twist at the end and uses some of the same high-frequency words repeatedly. Making your own books also allows you to create texts based on student interests, which will make rereading them even more engaging for children during reading time—*Star Wars*? *Frozen*? Horses? If you can't find a book on a topic children love, make one in an interactive writing group!

TAKE IT TO YOUR
CLASSROOM

- ✅ Take a closer look at some assessments that can help you shape the interactive writing lesson to have a maximum impact on your students (e.g., writing samples, letter identification, kidwatching, and more).

- ✅ Choose a group of children who would benefit from practicing a few of the same strategies.

- ✅ Think about the authentic purpose you'll offer them to begin the lesson.

- ✅ Remember: keep the amount of writing you'll do in the small group very short!

- ✅ Preplan. Although you will invite children to plan and orally rehearse what they want to write, you might preplan some text that will allow them to practice what you want them to practice. For example, if you want children to practice writing -ed and -ing endings, you'll have to make sure that some of the words you write together will have those spelling features.

- ✅ Think about which students will be involved with which aspects of the writing.

8

Inquiry Groups

Picture It: First Graders Study *Thank You, Omu!* by Oge Mora

"I know we loved this book, *Thank You, Omu!,* when we read it earlier this week," Ms. Washington begins as she gathers at a small table with four of her first graders. "We loved the story and the pictures . . . and I thought that today, we could revisit this book to help us with our *writing*." She explains how writers can study details in the pictures and in the words to get ideas for writing moves they can try in their own writing. Then she places the book on the table in front of the children so they can all see it.

Ms. Washington turns to the first page to give some examples, "I see that the author started with 'On the corner of First Street and Long Street, on the very top floor'—those are details about the setting, or the place the story is happening. That's one way to start a story. You can start *your* story by telling your readers where your story is happening, too!" She continues, "Let's see what else I can notice if I look closely. On the next page, I see the word *KNOCK!* in all caps. That's a sound word! We can use sound words in our writing, too. And look here! In this sentence, she uses *scrumptious*, *stove*, *scent*, *simmered*, *stew*, *street*—that's a lot of *s* words all in one sentence. I bet she did that on purpose—how does it make you feel when you hear all those /s/ sounds?"

Jude says, "It's like the steam coming off the soup!"

Ms. Washington then turns the noticing over to the group. She invites the students to talk with a partner about the next page. As they talk, Ms. Washington is actively involved, prompting the children to notice, name, and discuss what they see and why the author might have made the choices they did

STRATEGY
7.8

STRATEGY
9.6

STRATEGY
6.3

with questions such as, "What about these three dots? Those aren't on every page, are they? Why are they here? What might they mean?"

After the children get the hang of noticing and naming, she encourages them to talk about *why* and *when* they might try what they've noticed in their own writing. When Siobhan says, "The characters are talking on this page," Ms. Washington prompts her with, "Yes! The author makes the characters talk. Why might Oge Mora have done that, do you think?" When Siobhan responds that it helps you get to know the characters, Ms. Washington asks, "Might you try that in your writing?" Siobhan says that she's already done that, and Dylan chimes in that he wants to give it a try on the page of his book where he first sees the roller coaster. As the students continue, they find a number of things to notice, name, and possibly try, and Ms. Washington summarizes their conversation on a craft chart for easy reference (Ray 1999).

After about twelve minutes of noticing, naming, charting, and thinking together, Ms. Washington wraps up the group with a send-off naming what they might try today, and with a bigger idea about the power of studying others' writing in general: "Remember, you can always turn to other authors' work for inspiration and ideas that can help you with your own writing!"

Thank You, Omu! Craft Chart

What We Notice	Example	why? when?
setting	"On the corner of First St..."	Tell the reader where the story is happening to help them picture it.
words that start with the same sound	scrumptious simmered stove stew scent street	Give a feeling to match what's happening.
sound words	KNOCK!	Helps the reader feel like they're there.
• • • (ellipses)	... a little boy	To build suspense
facial expressions	Grandma frowns.	shows character feelings.
repetition	"Thank you, Omu."	• Matches the title. • Matches the most important part.
italics	delicious	Emphasis
describing words	thick big fat	To give more detail + help a reader picture it.

What Are Inquiry Groups?

Inquiry is an investigation, an act of asking a question and exploring possible answers. In writing inquiry groups, the essential question is: *What has this author done that we might want to try in our own writing?* This can be phrased in a more focused way aligned to a goal, such as: *How does this author make careful word choices in ways that I might want to try in my own writing?*

Rather than coming right out and answering the question for children (as you would in a strategy lesson), you guide them to notice and name craft in a mentor or touchstone text and consider its purpose. In inquiry groups, you support children as they discover, and help to trigger their curiosity. This approach can lead to increased engagement and can make the takeaways more memorable (Buchanan et al. 2016).

Inquiry groups are not completely open-ended; you play an important role in selecting the children for the group (likely a group of children who are working on a common goal) and selecting a text to study written by a published author or another student (likely a text they are already familiar with as readers). Your role in expertly guiding children during the lesson is also crucial—sometimes you'll guide children with *what* to notice, pointing out particular parts, pages, structures, features, or punctuation; sometimes with *what to make of* what they notice, coaching them to consider purpose and when or why an author might use a particular strategy or technique. You may also act as scribe, collecting what they notice and the ideas about what they notice on a common chart.

Inquiry groups are versatile. They can help writers working to get the basics of a genre such as organizing a story with a beginning, middle, and end; with studying illustrations; with writing a sentence with ending punctuation; and so on. They are also a great way to ramp up the craft for students who seem to be doing it all and whose writing is outpacing your whole-class lessons: pull them together to notice the

Some Advantages of Inquiry-Based Learning

- ✓ Piques curiosity
- ✓ Deepens understanding
- ✓ Fosters ownership
- ✓ Allows for differentiation
- ✓ Teaches a habit of mind

Key Terms

Mentor text. Usually selected by the student, this is a piece of writing that the writer aspires to emulate. Writers might refer back to the text as they compose, trying out different techniques, and using it as a model.

Touchstone text. Usually selected by the teacher and used repeatedly throughout a unit of study, this is a piece of writing that serves as an example of what students will be learning. What the writer does in the touchstone text matches the grade-level expectations, objectives, and/or standards. It is likely that a single touchstone text will yield many lessons or examples.

Who is this for? When do I choose inquiry groups?

Grade levels	Goals
✓ Pre-K	✓ Composing with pictures
✓ K	✓ Engagement
✓ 1	✓ Generating ideas
✓ 2	✓ Focus
✓ 3	✓ Organization/structure
✓ 4	✓ Elaboration
✓ 5	✓ Word choice
✓ 6	✓ Conventions: spelling
✓ 7	✓ Conventions: grammar and punctuation
✓ 8	✓ Partnerships and clubs

craft in a text they admire and see what jumps out at them.

Perhaps one of the most important goals of inquiry lessons is empowering students to do this on their own. Yes, they will learn about specific craft techniques in a specific text each time they study one with you. But the power of this lesson type transcends any specific craft techniques. In these lessons, they will learn about the *process by which* a writer learns from other writing. This is a skill they can take with them any time they are working on any piece in any genre.

conference

nquiry can be used as a method in one-to-one conferring, in small groups, and in whole-class lessons. You'll make a choice about how many students participate based on their individual goals and needs. The roles of teacher and student, as well as the moves the teacher makes, are the same no matter how many children are participating in the lesson. Watch this example of a conference with a fourth grader who studies paragraphing in a novel to make decisions about how to change the paragraphs in his work. As you view, take note that my role is to help name what he's noticing and to lead him through the inquiry.

STRATEGY 9.19

Video 8.1

See page xiii to access the online video.

Structure and Timing

In an inquiry lesson, you'll gather a group of children who are working on a common goal (i.e., elaboration, word choice, structure), although they needn't all be in need of the same strategy. You'll be studying a mentor text together through the lens of the goal, but you can guide children to notice a variety of craft techniques within that goal; each student might choose to try out different techniques, though they'll learn from what others notice and discuss during the lesson.

Learning through inquiry in a small group (rather than the whole class) gives each child in the group more opportunities to be involved and actively practice; this can be especially important for children who might get lost in a whole-class lesson. And in small-group inquiry lessons, you can align the text you study and the techniques to notice with what students need most.

How you start an inquiry group will depend on how much experience your students have studying mentor texts, but over time the goal is to spend the majority of your time supporting student's observations, helping them to name what they notice, and supporting them in considering author's purpose for what they notice.

Keep an eye on students' writing after inquiry lessons to see what transfers. Some children will be able to go from noticing straight to applying it in their own writing. For many children, the example isn't enough; they'll need a strategy. You could choose to end the *link* of the inquiry lesson with a clear strategy for one of the techniques you noticed. Alternatively (or in addition), you could use this inquiry lesson as the springboard to a series of future lessons that reference the example and mentor text and that move to specify *how* to try different techniques in their own writing.

HOW MUCH SUPPORT?

Your role in an inquiry group is to act as a guide on the side, prompting and leading children to discover examples of craft in text. Since you are not articulating the strategy to practice up front and instead are looking for them to do the discovering, this type of group typically offers students a *light* amount of support. You can increase the amount of support by offering more leading prompts and questions, or by demonstrating or giving examples before students practice or while they're practicing.

Inquiry Lessons Go Like This:

1. **Establish a Purpose:** Remind students of their goal and explain the focus for studying the mentor text. If this is the first time they've been engaged in a lesson like this, explain what it means to *read like a writer*—reading for craft and writing style, rather than *reading like a reader*—reading for information or entertainment. You may also offer a quick example or two, especially if this practice and procedure is new.

2. **Coach:** Guide student observations of a text or a series of short excerpts of texts. Students can either look at one physical copy all together or can each mark up their own copies. As you coach, you might point out what you want them to notice ("What about this part?"), guide them to name what they see ("What might we call this?"), and/or guide their thinking about purpose ("Why would an author choose to do it that way?"). The majority of the lesson is spent here, in the guided practice. When students notice things that aren't connected to their goal, refocus them on the lesson objective. Listen for opportunities to support students with naming or considering the author's purpose (see "Prompts that help students consider purpose" on page 131). It's a good idea to capture the conversation in a chart, perhaps like the one shown earlier in this chapter (page 120).

3. **Link:** Remind students what they noticed and invite them to try some techniques in their own writing, right away, if they match their purpose. Also remind them that studying a mentor text is something they can do on their own, anytime!

Tip

Be open to being pleasantly surprised! There's a good chance that during these lessons *you'll* learn *from* your students. Students often notice and get excited about something in a text that I hadn't paid attention to as I was planning and that I wasn't going to teach. But once they point it out, I'll often revise my unit in response, weaving a more explicit mention about it into a future whole-class or small-group lesson.

FAQ: How do I know which text(s) to choose for students to study?

Important question! The success of the small group hinges partially on making sure the text(s) you choose to study together matches what the students in the group would benefit from learning. If the students in the group are writing in more sophisticated ways than the mentor text you're studying, it's likely they won't grow much from the experience. If the text is in the wrong genre or doesn't offer a lot of examples for what students are looking to get better at, their time might be better spent back at their seats independently writing.

One of the best ways to set yourself up to be successful is to read children's books regularly and work to collect a small set of books that are rich with craft, that you love, and that you'll return to again and again. I have curated six collections of fifteen books, unique to each grade K–5, that can be found online (akj-education.com/akj-education-jennifer-serravallo-writing-collections-1). A quick search with terms such as "mentor text Padlet" or "mentor texts for narrative writing" will turn up many other teachers' lists of favorites.

In addition to considering the writing skills and craft a mentor text offers, it is also important to consider representation. Gholdy Muhammad (2020) challenges us to consider how everything we do in the classroom is a conscious choice, including the texts we select to use in instruction that can help to combat racism and bias. According to Lee and Low's (2020) recent analysis of children's literature, publishing is largely white: from the authors to editors, from the illustrators to the featured characters. (See the 2019 results: blog.leeandlow.com /2020/01/28/2019diversitybaselinesurvey/.) Rudine Sims Bishop has helped us to understand the importance of disrupting the status quo by diversifying our book selections. One of the crucial reasons to do this is so that Indigenous children, Black children, and all children of color see themselves in the texts (she calls this "mirrors"), to communicate that they are valued, to help them engage with reading and writing, and for so many other reasons. But it is also crucial for white students; when white children only see themselves in the books we use, they could grow up assuming that white people are most important, which is of course a dangerous message to send (Bishop 1990).

If you need help finding your way to great books that represent the diversity of the world and are also examples of excellent writing, I recommend scanning annual awards lists such as the Pura Belpré Awards, Stonewall Book Awards, Coretta Scott King Book Awards, American Indian in Youth Literature Awards, and Asian/Pacific American Award for Literature, to name a few. For years, Tricia Ebarvia, Dr. Kim Parker, Lorena German, and Julia Torres have been leading the way with their #DisruptTexts Twitter chats, website, blogs, and conference presentations. Their mission is to disrupt what is considered to be the "cannon" for middle and high school English classrooms and instead "create more inclusive, representative language arts curriculum" (disrupttexts.org). This is something we can all do.

If you need help with examples of what strategies can be taught with specific texts, there are also a number of professional books that focus on the power of studying published and student writing. Here are some I have in my collection:

Wondrous Words, Katie Wood Ray

A first-of-its-kind book from 1999 that explains how to teach children to learn to write from their reading and offers many examples of children's books and how they might be used. Given the publication date of this professional text, expect many of the children's books mentioned to be classics you may already have in your collection.

The Writing Thief and *Dream Wakers,* Ruth Culham

Culham offers examples of texts that can be used to teach about what she calls "The 6 Traits," qualities of good writing. *Dream Wakers* features books by and about Latinx people and includes 120 texts (half of which are bilingual or are available in English and Spanish editions) with lesson ideas for each.

The Big Book of Details, Rozlyn Linder

This book focuses on the goal of elaboration, and each chapter offers lesson ideas and examples from children's literature for types of and/or reasons for a variety of details. For each lesson idea, Linder excerpts three or four sentences or phrases to use as an example. During an inquiry lesson, it could be interesting to look across several short examples rather than within a single longer text, or you could choose one of the excerpts she offers and look at the whole text.

Craft Moves, Stacey Shubitz

In this book, Shubitz chooses twenty recently published children's books and shows how they can be used to teach 180 lessons. This makes the book very practical but also shows the power of a small, curated collection that can be used for a wide variety of purposes, which hopefully inspires you to find what *your* favorite collection of books will be.

In Pictures and In Words, Katie Wood Ray

If you work with young writers, get this book and you will never look at an illustration in a children's book the same way—or teach children about drawing in the same way. Ray covers perspective, showing movement, crafting background, and much more, using student examples and examples from published picture books.

Patterns of Power series, Jeff Anderson and Whitney LaRocca

Jeff Anderson has been writing for years about the power of mentor sentences to teach grammar and punctuation decisions, and his new series of work with Whitney LaRocca offers sentences culled from a wide variety of children's literature organized into grammar and punctuation techniques.

Learning from Classmates, Lisa Eickholdt

In this book, Lisa Eickholdt shows how other students can serve as mentors and models. Student work that is included might be used in your own classroom, and you will also get ideas for what to look for in your own students' pieces so they can become mentors, too!

Writing with Mentors, Allison Marchetti and Rebekah O'Dell

In this book, high school educators Marchetti and O'Dell focus on helping students find current, engaging mentor texts to help widen a sense of audience beyond school. They give many examples along the way of texts that are accessible via online link. This book is more than just lists of texts, though, as the authors empower readers to understand how the texts can be used in high school (and maybe even middle school) across the writing process. The authors also have a great curated collection on their website, movingwriters.org (search for "Mentor Text Dropbox").

Pause and Watch

Video 8.2

See page xiii to access the online video.

Pause your reading to watch a video of an inquiry group with three seventh graders who are writing memoir and fiction.

Here are some important teaching moves to notice as you watch the lesson:

✓ Before this group began, I sent all the students a link to download the text (some printed it, some had it on-screen during the lesson) and a short video of me reading it to ensure they could all access it.

✓ I use a document camera to display a craft chart in progress to keep track of what students notice.

STRATEGIES
5.19, 6.20,
9.31, 6.45

✓ The first comments from the children are somewhat vague: "The details are specific" and "He goes on and on." I redirect them by naming and modeling ways to talk about writing.

✓ I try not to point too much out to them during the first half of the group—I leave it open-ended to see what they are able to notice.

✓ As the group proceeds, I offer a little more direction by pointing out something that the children aren't naturally noticing (rhythm/pace of sentences and varying sentence length).

✓ Wait time! I try to wait it out after giving a prompt to encourage students to participate.

✓ At the end of the lesson, I reiterate some of the main takeaways from the specific text we looked at together and suggest they look at some of their favorite books with this lens.

WHAT WE NOTICE	EXAMPLE	WHY? WHEN?
Setting the scene	Age, place	1st sentence
Shock the reader	"My mother threw me out of a moving car."	Keep reader's attention
Culture, identity, background	"black South African" "christian"	Tell more about main character
Short sentences	"Tue. night was..." "Wed. night was..."	Faster pace, keeps you reading
Hints/mystery/ show not tell	Doesn't tell feelings	Keep reader curious
Emphasis	Never — and still is — adopt... adopt...adopt	Gives it importance

Craft Chart from Studying Page 1 of Trevor Noah's *Born a Crime*

FAQ: What are some common ways teachers prompt students during an inquiry lesson?

In an inquiry lesson, your role is to *guide* and empower students to be the ones noticing, naming, and thinking. It's important to keep an eye on how much support you offer and to be mindful that although there may be times when you need to give an example, you don't want all of the talking to come from you. The more you can prompt children and elicit their ideas, the more independent and empowered they will be to try this on their own.

I find that my prompts tend to fall into a few predictable categories:

PROMPTS THAT HELP POINT TO CRAFT ALIGNED TO THE STUDENTS' GOAL

I use these prompt types when students are noticing things that they already do as writers or when what they notice isn't connected to the focus of the inquiry. For example, imagine a group of students who are supposed to be noticing how a piece is organized, but are pointing out the ellipses.

- "We're thinking about [goal]. Let's look for examples in the text."

- "What are some things you notice [author] is doing that might help you with your goal of [name goal]?"

- "Yes, I notice that too. Let's tuck that one away since it doesn't go with the goal of [name goal] and come back to it another time."

- "Let's all take a look at this spot. I think this will help you with [goal]."

PROMPTS THAT HELP STUDENTS NAME WHAT THEY OBSERVE

Sometimes what your students notice will have an official writerly term (i.e., show, not tell, or sentence fragment) and other times it won't. Sometimes you'll want them to know the term, but sometimes it can be fun and engaging for writers to call it whatever will help them to remember it.

- "What should we call this?"

- "This is called [writer's term]."

- "I'm not sure this has an official name, but let's give it one to help us remember. Who has an idea?"

PROMPTS THAT HELP STUDENTS CONSIDER PURPOSE

When students are new to this type of study, they might be stuck on general or generic reasons for why authors make the choices they do. Expect a lot of "because it makes the writing better" and "because it sounds good." These prompts can help them think more specifically about an author's purpose.

- "Why do you think [author name] did this?"

- "What impact does it have on you as a reader?"

- "What's unique about this? How else could they have written this part?"

- "I think we can assume it was a choice for the writer to do it this way. Let's talk about why they might have done it this way."

- "You're right! We can't really know for sure why [author] did it. But what's a possible reason?"

Spin It: Student-Led Groups with Mentor Texts

In Chapter 4, you read about student-led strategy lessons. Inquiry groups are another great structure for students to support one another and to be empowered as experts in the classroom community. These groups will probably go best once students have had practice exploring mentor or touchstone texts with you and are comfortable with the process of reading like a writer.

Lots of students have favorite authors and mentor texts they return to again and again and know like the backs of their hands. Encourage them to advertise their expertise and give a shout-out to their favorite authors, announcing, "I'm an expert on Jacqueline Woodson's writing! Come learn some new tips about using metaphor by studying one of her picture books with me." You might dedicate a community bulletin board for these sorts of open invitations or give students time during a writing share or minilesson to offer their help. Some students might need a nudge from you to feel ready to lead a group, "You've been using this text so effectively to try out new techniques in your own writing. Do you think you'd be up for guiding some of your friends to notice what you've noticed?"

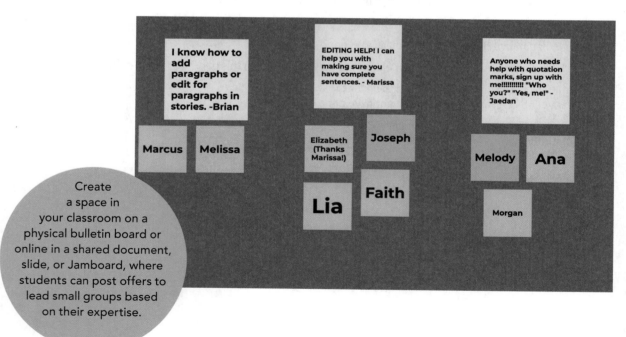

Create a space in your classroom on a physical bulletin board or online in a shared document, slide, or Jamboard, where students can post offers to lead small groups based on their expertise.

TAKE IT TO YOUR
CLASSROOM

✓ Explore your bookshelves, spend some time perusing book lists online, and/or pick up a professional text with ideas. Work on creating your own small collection of favorite texts that could be used again and again as mentors, and keep representation in mind as you do.

✓ Plan for a specific group of students. Likely the students will have a goal in common, and you'll want to find a text that will help them learn some new techniques.

✓ After teaching an inquiry lesson, reflect on how much support students needed to notice, name, and consider purpose. Reflect on the prompts you used. How might you prompt children in a future lesson with less support from you and with more independence (if possible)?

9

Reflection Groups

Picture It: Using Skill Progressions to Self-Assess Progress Toward Goals

"Writers, I've pulled you together today because you are both working on a goal of improving the elaboration, or detail, in your writing. I wanted to take a moment to guide your reflection: to celebrate all you've already learned and to look for areas where you might want some strategies to continue to grow. Let's start by taking a look at our skill progression for elaboration in opinion writing."

With the skill progression they've been using to guide their self-assessment on the table, Ms. Nguyen directs two fifth graders to take out their most recent drafts of persuasive letters. Focusing on one paragraph at a time, she coaches the students to notice and name what they are doing and to articulate their next steps.

Reasons supported (ex., info.)

Support is varied (quotes, anecdotes)

Support + why or How EXPLAIN...

Info = writer's knowledge PLUS research

She notices Mariel could use some help naming the kinds of details she's already included. "What's the reason you're writing about in this paragraph?" Ms. Nguyen begins. "And as you read some of the details you've included, ask yourself, 'Do my details support that reason?'" Mariel notices that three of her reasons do and one doesn't. Ms. Nguyen further prompts, "And of those details, would you say you're including examples, quotes, anecdotes, or something else?"

Mariel says that of the three that fit, they are all examples. "I notice I'm already writing a lot more details than I used to!" She looks back to the progression, "So I think I'm sort of here," she points to the progression and says, "I've got some supports. And I'm using examples. I need to make sure they all match and then maybe I can learn a strategy for a new kind of detail." Ms. Nguyen promises she's got a strategy that can help with that and directs her to check her next paragraph to see if her work is consistent throughout the piece.

Daniel easily identifies what he's already doing and what he needs to do, "I have a lot of different kinds of details." He points to sentences as he continues, "Here, I've got a quotation from an interview. Here, I've used a statistic. Here, I've got a list of a couple of examples. So I've gotten better about using different kinds of details. But I sort of just throw all the examples on the page. I'm not really explaining how they are proof. I think I need to work on that."

Ms. Nguyen checks back in with Mariel who has examined her second paragraph while her teacher was with Daniel. "This paragraph is better, I think," she says, "All my examples fit with the reason." Ms. Nguyen agrees with her reflection and offers her a strategy to work on for including a new type of detail to add more variety to her writing.

Next, she explains a quick strategy to Daniel to help him unpack or explain the details he includes.

"I want you both to highlight the part of the progression that shows what you're working on now. When I meet with you one-on-one later today or tomorrow, I'll give you some more help with the strategy I just gave you."

STRATEGY
6.33

Ms. Nguyen quickly jots a strategy for Mariel to help her vary her details. She asks her to find facts that need more elaboration and then choose which type of extra sentence (example, definition, story) might work best (Serravallo 2017).

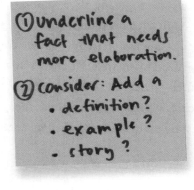

Daniel learns a different strategy, based on what he needs.

STRATEGY
6.23

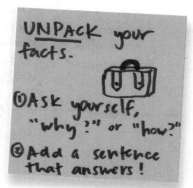

What Is a Reflection Group?

According to John Hattie (2008), "Effective feedback answers these questions: Where am I going (goal), How am I going (self-assessment and self-evaluation), Where to next (skill progression)" (176–77). Reflection groups give students the opportunity to evaluate their own work to set new goals or to evaluate their work in light of an existing goal to determine where they are and where they could go next. They also give teachers an excellent opportunity to get feedback *from* students. Watching students self-evaluate tells teachers what students understand about their goal and how well they are able to identify their own markers of success.

Lavery found that strategies are incredibly powerful, but they are most effective when they are focused on goal setting and planning and when children have a chance to self-instruct and self-evaluate (Hattie 2008). This means that the strategies you offer will be more meaningful, relevant, and impactful when students have regular opportunities to reflect and take stock of how they are doing, with guidance from you. Reflection empowers and motivates students,

A goal-setting conference is a one-on-one opportunity to meet with a student to guide their self-assessment, help them to reflect, and set a goal. If leading students through reflection and setting goals is new to you and/or your students, you may want to begin trying it one-on-one in a conference first, and then move to a small group once you and your students have the hang of it. To see an example, watch this goal-setting conference with a fourth-grade writer. Notice my role in supporting her reflection and practice: redirecting her, asking her to back up what she says with an example from her writing, and offering a strategy and support in practicing the strategy.

Video 9.1

See page xiii to access the online video.

STRATEGY 10.12

conference

Who is this for? When do I choose reflection groups?

Grade levels	Goals
√ Pre-K	√ Composing with pictures
√ K	√ Engagement
√ 1	√ Generating ideas
√ 2	√ Focus
√ 3	√ Organization/structure
√ 4	√ Elaboration
√ 5	√ Word choice
√ 6	√ Conventions: spelling
√ 7	√ Conventions: grammar and punctuation
√ 8	√ Partnerships and clubs

and it helps them develop a habit of mind that you hope carries beyond the specific meeting: that when working to improve, it's important to regularly reflect, celebrate, and look ahead to what's next.

When you pull together a small group of students for the purpose of reflection, goal setting, and/or self-assessment, the students in the group will likely have something in common—such as a common goal—to make your coaching easier to manage. Reflection groups can be helpful for any grade level and for students working on any goals.

Structure and Timing

In a reflection group, you'll guide students to study their work to articulate where they are and where they might go. You'll want to make sure to prompt them to celebrate their successes and also to help them with concrete plans for next steps. Reflection groups last around ten minutes, less if there are only two children in the group, and maybe slightly longer with a larger group.

To start, ask students to gather up the work that will be most helpful for them to see what you want them to see (you'll need to know what work that is and tell them what to grab) and bring it to the group. You might also bring (or ask students to bring) other tools—rubrics, skill progressions, touchstone texts—that will be helpful for the reflection you've planned.

IF THE STUDENT WILL BE REFLECTING ABOUT . . .	THEN I'D PREPARE OR ASK THE STUDENT TO BRING . . .
How the details they've used in their essay match up with their thesis statement	Their most current draft
Working on better engagement during writing to improve their daily output	A week's worth of writing in a folder (K–2) or notebook (3–8)
Their punctuation choices	A recent draft or notebook entry A sample exemplar piece A checklist or skill progression
How much progress they've made toward their goal	Work from the last few weeks, showing progress A skill progression focused on their goal
Improving conversation and collaboration during a writing club meeting	A video, audio recording, or transcript of a recent club meeting

You'll pull students together to set the intention for the group, coach them as they reflect, offer a strategy when appropriate, and make a promise for follow-up.

In a reflection group, you are leading children through self-reflection on their work, often anchored by a model text, rubric, and/or skill progression. Since the students are responsible for discovering where they are and what they might work toward next (with your guidance and support), this tends to offer a *light to moderate* amount of support. You can be more directive and give feedback about what you see the student needs if you need to increase the amount of support within the group.

Reflection Groups Go Like This:

1. **Set a Purpose:** Welcome students to the group and briefly explain what they'll be thinking about with you during the group meeting (i.e., setting a new goal or checking on progress with their current goal). Introduce or remind them of any materials or tools they might be using to support their reflection (i.e., rubrics, checklists, exemplar texts).

2. **Coach:** Although the students are in the group because they have something in common (i.e., they are working toward the same goal, or they are all ready for a new goal, or they are all at the same stage of the writing process), they are each unique writers. The coaching phase gives you the chance to check in with each student individually and tailor feedback to what they need. As you coach, make sure children are celebrating their growth and also articulating next steps. If you've chosen any materials or tools to support their reflection, this is when you use them. You may also introduce a strategy for each individual related to their goal, as is appropriate when you're working with them one-on-one.

3. **Link:** Remind students of their next steps and any strategy you've offered, and then promise a timely follow-up to provide them with more support.

Pause and Watch

Pause your reading to watch a video of a reflection group with three seventh graders who reflect on their poetry and set goals for future work.

Here are some teaching moves to notice as you watch the lesson:

✅ Before the group, direct each student to bring a recent sample of writing to base their reflection on, so they are prepared.

✅ I focus on five goals (rather than all ten) that are most likely to be useful, based on what I already know about the four writers' poetry writing.

✅ I name each of the five goals in kid-friendly language, and I explain a bit about why they might choose the goal and what questions to ask of themselves and their work.

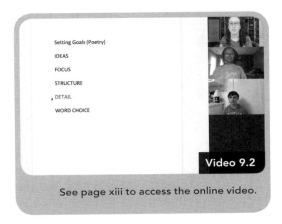

See page xiii to access the online video.

✅ I work with each writer on-one-one. Each student is in charge of their reflection, and I act as a support/guide.

✅ I offer each student a quick strategy after they choose their goal—I know that just naming a strategy without practicing it won't be enough support for all the students; I need to have a plan to follow up with them soon to support them with some guided practice.

STRATEGIES
4.20, 3.3,
4.19

What Can I Work On as a Writer? A Self-Reflection Tool for Finding Goals

Dear Teacher,

I created this self-reflection tool to be used with students as you work to find and establish goals for each of them. I wanted to help you involve students in the goal-setting process by offering them the opportunity to identify with statements that align to different goals from the "Hierarchy of Writing Goals" in *The Writing Strategies Book* (Serravallo 2017, 3).

What you'll likely find in using this self-reflection tool is that some students are able to identify their strengths and needs with accuracy and ease, while others will need more guidance in reflecting on concrete work samples. Therefore, I encourage you to use this self-reflection alongside your own evaluation of formative assessments (on-demand writing samples, pieces of writing that have been through the writing process, transcripts of kids working in partnerships or writing clubs, kidwatching during independent writing time, etc.) and steer and guide each student to what they need most if their own self-reflection seems out of sync with other information.

Here's how you may use this tool:

1. Ask stude...
2. After th... cuss to... potenti... hierar... There... I wou...
3. Ask... nee... giv...
4. Co... be...
5. E...

For students who could use more support, you... ...ts in the class as they refle... ...ence, bu...

See page xiii to access the online resources.

Self-Reflection Possibilities for Small Groups

Students might:

- Use a form with guiding questions to reflect on their work and consider what goal to choose.

This self-reflection form can be found in the online resources. Use it as is, or adapt it by decreasing the number of goals a student might consider. Modify the questions and prompts to be more unit focused if you wish. You can set students up to do their reflection independently, or use the questions during the small-group meeting.

- Use a rubric or success criteria to reflect on their work and consider what goal to choose.

This sample single-point rubric encourages children to reflect using a series of criteria aligned to their individual or unit goals. The skill progressions for each goal provided in the online resources can be adapted into single-point rubrics.

PUNCTUATION IN FICTION WRITING SINGLE-POINT RUBRIC

I need some help	Criteria	I can do it on my own
	Uses quotation marks correctly to punctuate dialogue	
	Uses midsentence punctuation (commas, dashes, semicolons) correctly	
	Uses paragraphs	

- Compare their work against a student-authored or teacher-authored exemplar, or published mentor, or touchstone text, and use it to set goals or to decide on new steps to take *within* a goal. (See Chapter 8 for more on studying mentor or touchstone texts.)

- Reflect on their work *within* their current goal, using a skill progression, and decide what their next steps are.

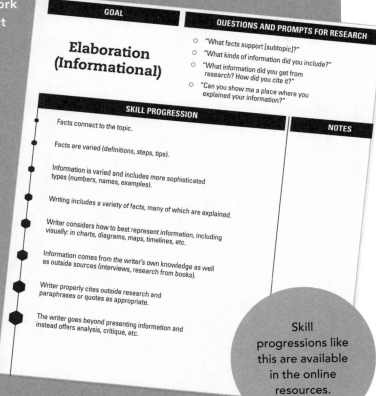

GOAL

Elaboration (Informational)

QUESTIONS AND PROMPTS FOR RESEARCH

○ "What facts support [subtopic]?"
○ "What kinds of information did you include?"
○ "What information did you get from research? How did you cite it?"
○ "Can you show me a place where you explained your information?"

SKILL PROGRESSION

Facts connect to the topic.

Facts are varied (definitions, steps, tips).

Information is varied and includes more sophisticated types (numbers, names, examples).

Writing includes a variety of facts, many of which are explained.

Writer considers how to best represent information, including visually: in charts, diagrams, maps, timelines, etc.

Information comes from the writer's own knowledge as well as outside sources (interviews, research from books).

Writer properly cites outside research and paraphrases or quotes as appropriate.

The writer goes beyond presenting information and instead offers analysis, critique, etc.

NOTES

Skill progressions like this are available in the online resources.

See page xiii to access the online resources.

- Reflect on their work and decide whether they've made adequate progress within their goal and if it's time to set a new goal.

- Watch a video or listen to an audio recording of themselves as they work in a partnership or club, and then reflect on how they can support their peers.

FAQ: Are there predictable prompts and questions you use to guide student observation of their own work?

Yes, I try as much as possible to be open-ended when I prompt so the child does the self-reflection work. My tendency is to start with lower-support prompts and work my way up to more support if I notice they need it.

"I'm going to give you a strategy today. What would you like to be able to do as a writer?"

"What seems like a good next step for you?"

"I notice that here [pointing to a part of their piece] you've tried _____ [looking at the skill progression/exemplar]. What seems like a next step?"

"Your goal is _____. What are some examples of what you've tried as you're working on that?"

"What can you notice you've improved on?"

"One thing I notice is _____. What do you think about that?"

"How does your work compare to the skill progression?"

"What do you see this author doing [gesture to a part of an exemplar] that you might want to try?"

TAKE IT TO YOUR
CLASSROOM

✓ A helpful reflection group begins with a teacher assessment before the group begins. You'll want to make sure you have a sense of what you'll be guiding students to see or notice about their work. You might assess during a conference or prior small group, read their writing on your own, and/or observe them during a conversation about their writing with peers.

✓ Form groups of students who are all working toward the same goal, ready for a new goal, or working at the same step of the process (i.e., revision) and are ready for a new strategy.

✓ Notice how much support and prompting students need to identify their goal or make growth according to a progression. Use this as a chance to get feedback *from* students about how much they understand about their goal, the genre they are working on, or the strategies you've shared with them. Students who seem to have a fuzzy understanding about what strong work looks like, or what they will be able to do when they've accomplished their goal, may benefit from an inquiry group to study exemplar writing in more depth (see Chapter 8).

✓ Take notes on what you discuss with students and jot down any strategy you offer to each one aligned to their goal during the small-group lesson. You'll want to be sure to follow up soon after this meeting to offer more guidance with the writing strategy, since most of this group meeting is about reflecting.

10

Partnerships
and Clubs

Picture It: A Sixth-Grade Songwriting Club

Lila and Sajiv are enthusiastic members of the school chorus who sing just about all day long. They started making up their own songs during recess, and just recently, decided to formalize their songwriting by writing their lyrics down. Their friend Phoebe, a TikTok enthusiast, doesn't love to sing as much as they do but has agreed to contribute by filming their music videos. Their teacher, Ms. Gabay, encouraged the three of them to spend time together during the writing class period to work on their songs and promised them some support from time to time.

One Friday afternoon, they meet in a corner of the classroom behind the bookshelf, and Ms. Gabay comes over to see if she can offer them any support. She sees their laptops open, a shared Google Doc on each of their screens, and song lyrics in the document. Phoebe is contributing ideas here and there to the song lyrics they are taking turns writing and is adding comments in the margins about what sorts of imagery to use in the music video to accompany the song. Ms. Gabay notes that they are working collaboratively, are deeply engaged, and are being productive, and they likely don't need support with any protocols for how to work together or strategies for functioning well as a club. Instead, she decides to look closely at the quality of the writing they are doing to see if they could benefit from a writing strategy to improve it. She gets close enough to read what's on the screen, and she listens in to the challenges they are trying to solve now.

"But I'm just not sure if it makes sense," Lila says, pointing to a line in the second part of their song.

"True, but it rhymes and fits the beat." Sajiv replies.

"Hm. OK, let's move on," Lila says.

Ms. Gabay jumps in, "Lila and Sajiv, I notice you're checking over some of the lines in your song to revise them, and you're wise to be making sure that the lines make sense. I see that you have a focus for your song. So one of the things you can do when you read through is to make sure each line *matches the focus* of the song. And if it doesn't, then you can try to reword what you're trying to say a few times until you find just the right words. Get the words right to match your meaning, then play with the words to get the right rhythm and rhyme. Meaning first, rhythm and rhyme second. Let's try together."

Ms. Gabay prompts them, keeping the strategy in mind ("How else can you say that?" "Try some other words." "Phoebe, what is it they're really trying to say in this part of the song? What image are you seeing for the video?" "OK, now let's play with the words so they rhyme"), and they work on rephrasing the line several times before they feel like it's just right.

STRATEGY
4.11

Ms. Gabay ends the meeting and reminds them that as they read through the rest of this song, and with the next song they write, it is important to keep the focus of the song in mind as they revise and to reword lines several times until the meaning, rhythm, and rhyme are all right.

Song lyrics to I Am A Girl

You said I'm not as good as you but that's clearly not true
Some people will believe whatever you say but what you say is not you
You don't need to be rude because I am the same as you
I am more than just your maid and i can do the things you do

I am a girl and I am proud
You need treat me like everyone else
I am a girl and I am strong
I can do everything you can
I am a girl
Oh I am a girl

I can climb mountains I can chop trees
I can hunt bears and I can skin knees
I can get dirty I can get in fights
It will do you good if you just are nice
She is just the same as he
Everything is equal in this world and if you don't care then you will see
what your words and actions do to me
You know it still matters if it's me it's not your choice but it still means to me

Lila and
Sajiv's Song
Lyrics Draft

What Are Partnerships and Clubs?

While you are working to support students to be independent writers, the truth is that all writers—even professional writers who do much of their writing independently!—still lean on others regularly and throughout their writing process. You can help nurture relationships in the classroom by providing time and structures for children to work together as writers, and in doing so, help to formalize relationships between peers in the classroom, turning an activity that is often solitary into something social and interactive. "Promoting learning together . . . cognitively and emotionally sharing thoughts, ideas, and understanding in a collaborative fashion, has significant potential for increased comprehension and learning" (Howard, Milner-McCall, and Howard 2020, 15).

Writing partnerships are pairs of students who work together to support one another's writing and work throughout the writing process. All students in the class can be paired up with a writing partner. You'll usually choose who to match up (though eliciting ideas from students for who would work well together is wise). Partners work best when they can each learn something from the other, but where their overall writing levels are not drastically different.

Writing clubs are student run and are usually student initiated. Clubs are often formed from a common interest: a group who want to work together to write a play, or study a mentor text, or give and get feedback. Clubs often form when children are interested in working on side projects that are independent and outside of the class unit of study, though a club could also form to take a class unit in a different direction

Who is this for? When do I choose partnerships and clubs?

Grade levels	Goals
✓ Pre-K	✓ Composing with pictures
✓ K	✓ Engagement
✓ 1	✓ Generating ideas
✓ 2	✓ Focus
✓ 3	✓ Organization/structure
✓ 4	✓ Elaboration
✓ 5	✓ Word choice
✓ 6	✓ Conventions: spelling
✓ 7	✓ Conventions: grammar and punctuation
✓ 8	✓ Partnerships and clubs

Ways that Children Can Support Each Other as Writers in Partnerships or Clubs

- Brainstorm ideas for what to write about (topics) or how to write about topics (forms or genres).

- Rehearse aloud and give feedback during rehearsals.

- Help to get unstuck when writer's block hits.

- Help to problem solve when something isn't working.

- Give feedback and revision suggestions—on structure, tone, details, word choice, and more.

- Ask critical questions about parts that are confusing, unclear, or need more elaboration.

- Co-write a piece.

- Ask for or give advice.

- Compliment and cheerlead their peers as they work through challenges, accomplish a goal, finish a piece.

- Hold peers accountable for something they promised to try or to work on.

- Provide expertise to compensate for individual weak spots.

(i.e., during a fiction unit a group of children want to publish their stories as graphic novels).

Although partnerships and clubs can be a valuable way for students to support one another across the process (see sidebar at left), we can't just put children into groups without any support or instruction and expect that they will all have routines for working together, or have strategies for offering feedback to one another in respectful and helpful ways. Conferring with peer groups positions you as a coach who helps them have productive positive experiences working together.

Different from all other small groups, you don't select students to work with in partnerships or clubs—the groups are already formed. Whether students are all meeting in spots around the classroom simultaneously during a "partner/club time," or select partners and clubs meet on different days in a designated meeting spot in the room, you can make sure to check in, give positive feedback, and offer a strategy to support them.

It is likely that each individual student in the partnership or club will have their own goals, so, unlike other groups that you form based on a common need, in partnership and club instruction you have to decide whose individual goal to support with a strategy (if you are teaching into writing quality) or to support them all with partnership/club routines or behaviors.

Structure and Timing

Most partnership and club small-group lessons begin with quiet observation. You'll sit alongside the students, careful to keep their attention on one another and not on you. Of course, if you come to observe a group and nothing is happening, you can begin your lesson by offering them a strategy to get working together.

As students co-write, give feedback, listen to each other, brainstorm together, and so on, listen in and consider the kind of strategy that would be most helpful. Your goal is to teach them something that will help them help each other as writers and that will allow them to work with independence when you're not nearby. You might choose:

A strategy that teaches them a *procedure* for working together	For example, teaching them to sit side by side, with both eyes on the same physical page. One writer reads their work aloud, and the listening partner politely pauses their partner after every paragraph/page to say something.
A strategy that supports them with *the craft of writing*	For example, teaching them how to scan the writing for types of detail (action, dialogue, thinking), notice what the piece could use more of, and make a suggestion for what to add.
A strategy that supports them with *collaboration and co-composing*	For example, teaching them how to draft a play together by first acting out a part, then pausing to write down what they've written. Then, after the first draft is written, act it out with script in hand and revise based on what's working and what's not.

HOW MUCH SUPPORT?

Partnerships and writing clubs will ideally be functioning with some level of independence, and your role is to observe and offer them a strategy to lift the level of their work together. In this scenario, the level of teacher support is *light*. However, if students need support getting started and sustaining conversation and collaboration, the level of teacher support increases.

Small-Group Instruction During Partnership and Club Meetings Goes Like This:

1. **Research:** Sit close enough to the children that you can hear clearly what they are saying and watch what they are doing. Take notes on your observations and try not to say anything or take over. If students start directing conversation to you, redirect them back to their peers (say, "Pretend I'm not here!"); your focus here is on seeing what they can do as a group, independently. (If the group doesn't appear to be working together at all, move to step 4!)

2. **Decide:** Choose one thing to compliment based on what you see them doing well and one thing to support them with that is a slight nudge forward.

3. **Compliment:** Clearly name what they are doing that's productive and supportive to their peers and to their writing.

4. **Teach:** Offer students a strategy to practice.

5. **Coach:** Stick around for a couple of minutes and offer support as they practice.

6. **Link:** Repeat the key takeaways from your time with them and name what you want to see them continue to practice.

Pause and Watch

Pause your reading to watch the videos of two writing partnerships: one with first graders and one with fourth graders.

As you watch, you might notice:

STRATEGY 10.12

✔ The lesson with the first graders begins with me teaching a strategy. As I observed from afar (before the lesson began), I saw the two students sitting next to each other, unsure how to start. If, instead, they had been engaged as partners often are, I would have watched them for a moment before jumping in with a compliment and strategy.

Video 10.1

See page xiii to access the online video.

✔ The first-grade partnership needs a lot of support—I give them sentence starters and coach them with many of the sentences they say. I hope that in future meetings, they can use this strategy with more independence. Still, this is a good example of how much support some children need when they first try this type of small group!

✔ In the fourth-grade group, I try to use the visual chart as a way to say less, and also as a way to get them to reference their tools. This will help them to be independent even after I leave.

Video 10.2

See page xiii to access the online video.

✔ In the fourth-grade group, when Maresh coaches her partner, the strategy is new, and they need a lot of support. Notice the difference when the roles are reversed and Maresh's partner is coaching her; they need much less support from me and do much more independently. Now that they have the hang of it, I hope they are able to continue without me there.

STRATEGY 10.10

"Does It Match My Intention?"

1. Tell your partner the most important thing about your piece:

THEME   MAIN IDEA   FEELING   FOCUS

2. Read your draft. Pause often. Ask:

"DO THESE DETAILS I READ FIT WITH MY FOCUS? WHAT MIGHT I CHANGE? ADD? DELETE?"

Barb Golub

MAKE PROMISES (YOU CAN KEEP)

1. Talk about your goals with your partner.

2. Plan how to meet it.

3. Plan a celebration. PARTY!!!

4. Check in soon.

How's it going?

Barb Golub

STRATEGIES 10.5, 10.11, 10.12

GOAL Supporting peer collaboration in partnerships and clubs

Help Your Writing Partner Add Details...
INTERRUPT and get more info...

SETTING
✓ Describe where it happened
✓ What did you see?
✓ What did you hear?

DIALOGUE
✓ What did he/she say?
✓ What were the exact words that came out of his/her mouth?

ACTION
✓ Back up, go slower
✓ What was the very next thing he/she did?
✓ Act it out!

THINKING
✓ What were you thinking?
✓ What was going through his/her head?

FEELING
✓ What were you feeling?
✓ Describe how that looks...

Interrupt Your Partner: Listen to your partner as they tell their story. As soon as you notice your partner is skipping some important information, gently interrupt with a prompt for more. Your partner will then rewind and storytell the same part, but include the information you asked for.

Sample Strategies for Supporting Partnerships and Clubs
Strategies are from The Writing Strategies Book *(Serravallo 2017).*

FAQ: How do I fit partnerships and clubs into my packed schedule?

Primary Classrooms

Children typically meet with their partner during each, or most, writing periods. This meeting may either be before writing independently (perhaps to brainstorm ideas or set a focus for their independent work for the day), after they are finished their independent writing for the day (perhaps to share what they worked on, get feedback on something, or celebrate something they tried), or during a brief midworkshop interruption (perhaps for a quick share and to refocus themselves for the remainder of the writing block).

Upper Elementary Classrooms

By third and fourth grades, children typically have more stamina for collaboration and conversation and more practice with partnership work. Therefore, you may set up a schedule where children meet less frequently but for longer periods of time (maybe once or twice a week for fifteen minutes) during the writing block.

Middle School Classrooms

Time is very short in middle school classrooms; usually there is barely enough time to teach writing and reading and give children time to practice both each day. In middle school classrooms, students might meet together once a week, for half or a quarter of the period, to provide more in-depth feedback and support. Briefer, more frequent check-ins could happen during quick turn-and-talks during minilessons or end-of-workshop teaching shares.

In classes at any grade level, you might consider setting up a partner space in your classroom where children can go, even when it isn't "partner time," when they could use support from a peer. You might put a five-minute sand timer or other silent timer in the area for them to self-monitor, and a sign-up sheet for kids who want to use the space next if it's occupied.

TAKE IT TO YOUR
CLASSROOM

✓ In partnerships, match your writers with peers who have complementary strengths and needs. Ideally each student has something to learn from the other, and they get along well and enjoy working together. Consider asking children who they prefer to be with and might work best with!

✓ Plan to teach some whole-class lessons that offer strategies or protocols. For example, the "Praise–Question–Polish" (PQP) protocol you saw in the video might be a great place to start for your students. For younger children, you may even need to discuss body language or how to actively listen first.

✓ Decide if you'll establish a partner time in each writing period or at certain times during the week, if you'll stagger the partner meetings on different days of the week so you can be there to meet with them, and/or if you'll set up a partner spot in the classroom where students can go with their partner at any time in the writing period.

✓ Share the concept of writing clubs with your class and give some examples of ways they might work with a club, if they choose.

Works Cited

Anderson, Carl. 2000. *How's It Going? A Practical Guide to Conferring with Student Writers*. Portsmouth, NH: Heinemann.

———. 2005. *Assessing Writers*. Portsmouth, NH: Heinemann.

Anderson, Jeff, and Whitney LaRocca. 2017. *Patterns of Power: Inviting Young Writers into the Conventions of Language, Grades 1–5*. Portsmouth, NH: Stenhouse.

Ascenzi-Moreno, L. 2018. "Translanguaging and Responsive Assessment Adaptations: Emergent Bilingual Readers Through the Lens of Possibility." *Language Arts* 95 (6): 355–69.

Baker-Bell, April. 2020. *Linguistic Justice: Black Language, Literacy, Identity, and Pedagogy*. New York: Routledge.

Bear, Donald, Marcia Invernizzi, Shane Templeton, and Francine Johnston. 2012. *Words Their Way: Word Study for Phonics, Vocabulary, and Spelling Instruction*. 5th ed. New York: Pearson.

Bishop, Rudine Sims. 1990. "Mirrors, Windows, and Sliding Glass Doors." *Perspectives: Choosing and Using Books for the Classroom* 6 (3): ix–xi.

Buchanan, Shelly Marie Crist, Mary Ann Harlan, Christine Bruce, and Sylvia Edwards. 2016. "Inquiry Based Learning Models, Information Literacy, and Student Engagement: A Literature Review." *School Libraries Worldwide* 22 (2): 23–39.

Calkins, Lucy. 1994. *The Art of Teaching Writing*. Portsmouth, NH: Heinemann.

———. 2014. *Writing Pathways. Performance Assessments and Learning Progressions, Grades K–8*. Portsmouth, NH: Heinemann.

Clay, Marie. 2017. *Concepts About Print*. 2nd ed. Portsmouth, NH: Heinemann.

Cohen and Steele. 2002. "A Barrier of Mistrust: How Negative Stereotypes Affect Cross-Race Mentoring." In *Improving Academic Achievement: Impact of Psychological Factors on Education*, edited by J. Aronson, 303–27. Academic Press.

Coppola, Shawna. 2019. *Writing Redefined: Broadening Our Ideas of What It Means to Compose*. Portsmouth, NH: Stenhouse.

Cruz, M. Colleen. 2004. *Independent Writing: One Teacher, 32 Needs, Topics, and Plans*. Portsmouth, NH: Heinemann.

Culham, Ruth. 2016a. *Dream Wakers: Mentor Texts That Celebrate Latino Culture*. Portsmouth, NH: Stenhouse.

———. 2016b. *The Writing Thief: Using Mentor Texts to Teach the Craft of Writing.* Portsmouth, NH: Stenhouse.

Eickholdt, Lisa. 2015. *Learning from Classmates: Using Students' Writing as Mentor Texts.* Portsmouth, NH: Heinemann.

España, Carla, and Luz Yadira Herrera. 2020. *En Comunidad: Lessons for Centering the Voices and Experiences of Bilingual Latinx Students.* Portsmouth, NH: Heinemann.

Fountas, Irene, and Gay Su Pinnell. 2000. *Guiding Readers and Writers: Teaching Comprehension, Genre, and Content Literacy.* Portsmouth, NH: Heinemann.

———. 2017. *Literacy Continuum: A Tool for Assessment, Planning, and Teaching.* Portsmouth, NH: Heinemann.

Freire, Paulo. 1998. *Teachers as Cultural Workers: Letters to Those Who Dare to Teach.* Boulder, CO: Westview Press.

Gannon, Kevin. 2020. "Assessing with Equity in Mind." www.grandviewcetl.org /assessing-with-equity-in-mind.

Graves, Donald. 1983. *Writing: Teachers and Children at Work.* Portsmouth, NH: Heinemann.

Hammond, Zaretta L. 2015. *Culturally Responsive Teaching and The Brain: Promoting Authentic Engagement and Rigor Among Culturally and Linguistically Diverse Students.* Thousand Oaks, CA: Corwin.

Hattie, John. 2008. *Visible Learning.* New York: Routledge.

Hattie, John, and Shirley Clarke. 2018. *Visible Learning Feedback.* New York: Routledge.

Hilliard, Asa G. 2002. "Language, Culture, and the Assessment of African American Children." In *The Skin That We Speak: Thoughts on Language and Culture in the Classroom*, edited by Lisa Delpit, Chapter 6. New York: The New Press.

Howard, Jaleel R., Tanya Milner-McCall, and Tyrone C. Howard. 2020. *No More Teaching Without Positive Relationships.* Portsmouth, NH: Heinemann.

Inoue, Asao B. 2019. "How Do We Language So People Stop Killing Each Other, or What Do We Do About White Language Supremacy?" Opening Session of CCCC Annual Convention, Pittsburgh, PA, March 14. www.youtube.com/wat ch?v=brPGTewcDYY&feature=youtu.be.

Jewell, Tiffany. 2018. *This Book Is Antiracist: 20 Lessons on How to Wake Up, Take Action, and Do the Work.* Minneapolis, MN: The Quarto Group.

Kay, Matthew R. 2020. "Finding the Courage to Be Specific About Systemic Racism in Education." *ASCD Inservice* (blog). June 9. https://inservice.ascd .org/finding-the-courage-to-be-specific-about-systemic-racism-in-education.

King, Stephen. 2000. *On Writing: A Memoir on Craft*. New York: Simon and Schuster.

Ladson-Billings, Gloria. 2009. *The Dreamkeepers: Successful Teachers of African-American Children*. San Francisco: Jossey-Bass.

Lee & Low Books. 2020. "Where Is the Diversity in Publishing? The 2019 Diversity Baseline Survey Results." *The Open Book Blog*. January 28. https://blog.leeandlow.com/2020/01/28/2019diversitybaselinesurvey.

Lifschitz, Jessica. 2016. "The Students Become the Teachers." *Crawling Out of the Classroom* (blog). May 12. https://crawlingoutoftheclassroom.wordpress.com/2016/05/12/the-students-become-the-teachers.

Linder, Rozlyn. 2016. *The Big Book of Details: 46 Moves for Teaching Writers to Elaborate*. Portsmouth, NH: Heinemann.

Marchetti, Allison, and Rebekah O'Dell. 2016. *Writing with Mentors: How to Reach Every Writer in the Room Using Current, Engaging Mentor Texts*. Portsmouth, NH: Heinemann.

McCarrier, Andrea, Gay Su Pinnell, and Irene C. Fountas. 2000. *Interactive Writing: How Language & Literacy Come Together K–2*. Portsmouth, NH: Heinemann.

Means, Barbara, and Michael S. Knapp. 1991. "Rethinking Teaching for Disadvantaged Students." In *Teaching Advanced Skills to At-Risk Students: Views from Research and Practice*, edited by Barbara Means, Carol Chelemer, and Michael S. Knapp, 1–26. San Francisco: Jossey-Bass.

Milner, H. Richard IV. 2010. *Start Where You Are But Don't Stay There: Understanding Diversity, Opportunity Gaps, and Teaching in Today's Classrooms*. 2nd ed. Cambridge, MA: Harvard Education Press.

Minor, Cornelius. 2018. *We Got This: Equity, Access, and the Quest to Be Who Our Students Need Us to Be*. Portsmouth, NH: Heinemann.

Mora, Oge. 2018. *Thank You, Omu!* New York: Little Brown and Company.

Morrell, Earnest. 2012. "Teachers as Critical Researchers: An Empowering Model for Urban Education." In *The Critical Qualitative Research Reader*, edited by Shirley Steinberg and Gaile Cannella, 364–79. New York: Peter Lang.

Muhammad, Gholdy. 2020. *Cultivating Genius: An Equity Framework for Culturally and Historically Responsive Literacy*. New York: Scholastic.

National Governors Association Center for Best Practices, Council of Chief State School Officers. 2010. *Common Core State Standards*. Washington, DC: National Governors Association Center for Best Practices, Council of Chief State School Officers.

Pearson, P. D., and G. Gallagher. 1983. "The Gradual Release of Responsibility Model of Instruction." *Contemporary Educational Psychology* 8: 112–23.

Ray, Katie Wood. 1999. *Wondrous Words. Writers and Writing in the Elementary Classroom*. Urbana, IL: NCTE.

———. 2000. *In Pictures and In Words: Teaching the Qualities of Good Writing Through Illustration Study*. Portsmouth, NH: Heinemann.

Ritchart, Ron. 2002. *Intellectual Character: What It Is, Why It Matters, and How to Get It*. San Francisco: Jossey Bass.

Routman, R. 2005. *Writing Essentials: Raising Expectations and Results While Simplifying Teaching*. Portsmouth, NH: Heinemann.

Sadler, D. Royce. 1989. "Formative Assessment and the Design of Instructional Systems." *Instructional Science* 18: 119–44.

Serravallo, Jennifer. 2010. *Teaching Reading in Small Groups*. Portsmouth, NH: Heinemann.

———. 2015. *The Reading Strategies Book*, Portsmouth, NH: Heinemann.

———. 2017. *The Writing Strategies Book*. Portsmouth, NH: Heinemann.

———. 2019a. *A Teacher's Guide to Reading Conferences*. Portsmouth, NH: Heinemann.

———. 2019b. *Understanding Texts & Readers*. Portsmouth, NH: Heinemann.

Shubitz, Stacey. 2016. *Craft Moves: Lesson Sets for Teaching Writing with Mentor Texts*. Portsmouth, NH: Stenhouse.

Souto-Manning, Mariana, Carmen I. Lugo Llerena, Jessica Martell, Abigail Salas Maguire, and Alicia Arce-Boardman. 2018. *No More Culturally Irrelevant Teaching*. Portsmouth, NH: Heinemann.

Souto-Manning, Mariana, and Jessica Martell. 2016. *Reading, Writing, and Talk: Inclusive Teaching Strategies for Diverse Learners, K–2*. New York: Teachers College Press.

Tomlinson, Carol Ann. 2001. *How to Differentiate Instruction in Mixed-Ability Classrooms*. 2nd ed. Alexandria, VA: Association for Supervision and Curriculum Development.

Zull, J. E. 2002. *The Art of the Changing Brain: Enriching the Practice of Teaching by Exploring the Biology of Learning*. Sterling, VA: Stylus.

978-0-325-07822-9

The Writing Strategies Book

Your Everything Guide to Developing Skilled Writers

In *The Writing Strategies Book*, Jen collects 300 of the most effective strategies to share with writers, grouping them within ten crucial goals. Each page comes alive with classroom charts or student work examples, mentor text suggestions, and lesson language.

An on-your-lap resource that helps you:

- identify goals for every writer

- give students step-by-step strategies for writing with skill and craft

- coach writers using prompts aligned to a strategy

- present mentor texts that support a genre and strategy

- adjust instruction to meet individual needs with Jen's Teaching Tips

- demonstrate and explain a writing move with her Lesson Language

- learn more with Hat Tips to the work of influential teacher–authors

- bring more joy to your classroom with dozens of ideas for writing celebrations

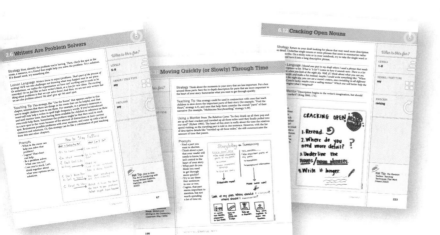

Scan here
to view a video about this book

Join Jennifer Serravallo Online

The Reading and Writing Strategies Facebook Group

Join Jen and 70,000 of your colleagues to discuss Jen's resources.

"I am thankful for this community and am a fairly new member. It has really helped me understand the reading and writing strategies better and how to implement them."

— Beverly Laird Hearn

Scan here to visit The Reading and Writing Strategies Facebook Group

The Heinemann Podcast

Listen to episodes of The Heinemann Podcast featuring Jen talking about topics such as:

- sustaining comprehension
- conferring
- how her books work together.

Scan here to visit the Heinmann Podca

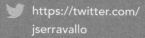

Twitter and Instagram

https://twitter.com/jserravallo

https://instagram.com/jenniferserravallo

Stay up to the minute on Jen's latest moves and thinking about teaching and the education issues of our time.